THE AUTHORITY
of the
PEOPLE of GOD

JEFFREY D. CRAWFORD

ALL PEOPLES MINISTRIES
LYNCHBURG, VA

The Authority of the People of God

Published by All Peoples Ministries
P.O. Box 3034
Lynchburg, Virginia 24503
www.allpeoplesministries.org

Copyright © 2022 Jeffrey D. Crawford

Cover design by Samuel C. Petty.

ISBN-13: 978-0-9987608-8-9

Printed in the United States of America

To God, the One true Authority in existence.

CONTENTS

FOREWORD

I was very honored when Jeff asked me to write the foreword to his book, *The Authority of the People of God*. It's also ironic to be endorsing a book that speaks to the very things I struggled to accept for most of my young adult years. I was pastoring a house church when I met Jeff in 2015. I found his church on the internet and sent him an email to connect for lunch. That was seven years ago, and now, we serve together in a local church. I am very fortunate to learn from his leadership, experience, and wisdom, but more so, I am fortunate to be his friend. He is one of the most down to earth, easy to talk to, caring, honoring, and genuine guys you will ever meet. God has entrusted him with a great deal of responsibility, both professionally and personally, and he has a long track record of success. I have never met anyone who talks more about the importance and benefits of biblical authority than Jeff. He is the most qualified person I know to write on this topic. I am very thankful God called him to pen his personal stories, paired with God's Word, on authority. It is a greatly deficient subject in today's culture and knowing how much Jeff values authority, I am excited to see the impact his book will have on the church body at large.

As a business owner, a consistent pet peeve of mine is opportunity loss. When we don't understand God's heart on authority, we leave money on the table, so to speak, so it's an opportunity loss. In business, the greater the risk, the greater the reward. It's the same with authority. When we risk our pride to honor authority, even when we disagree or our mind is offended, we position ourselves to experience a heavenly reward that will often catch us by surprise. As Jeff explains, the stakes are high because our God-given destiny is on the line. He explains that our ability to honor the authority figures God has strategically placed in our lives, will either set us up for great success, or set us on a path of destruction and failure.

Have you ever been mistreated by authority? Jeff shares how he was mistreated and how it all unfolded. It's one of my favorite chapters! Jeff's personal stories and the principles that he pulls from Scripture are life changing. God used this book as a tool in my own life for greater transformation and healing. I related to his stories because I too have been mistreated, by a previous pastor, but when I prayed about it, God asked me to willingly bear up under that mistreatment. It's not an easy thing to do, but Luke 6:28 tells us to pray for those who mistreat us. This type of godly response Christ desires will only come with a supernatural empowerment from the Holy Spirit and our willingness to accept the mission to love, even when it hurts. This is what following Jesus looks like. Count the cost!

Jeff shoots straight and doesn't mince his words. This book brought greater freedom and balance to my thinking about authority. He tells it like it is and backs it up with Scripture. He does a great job at laying a clear and biblical foundation through the historical narrative of Scripture and in sharing his personal stories and reminding the reader what our role is supposed to look like.

Be warned though: you may get triggered, like I was, while reading this book. I thought I was all good. I thought all my heart issues were healed in this area, but God has a way of peeling another layer of the onion. I wrestled with these truths and it challenged my perspective. Triggers are like the warning lights in the dash of your car, telling you something isn't operating correctly and you need a service repair. As Graham Cooke would say, God loves to hide upgrades in our circumstances. God will continue to allow life's circumstances to teach us not to bypass, ignore, or rebel against authority, and this book will shine a light on some of those areas not yet fully submitted or aligned with God's heart. Reading this book also challenged some of my perspectives regarding our own democratic government and all its systems, and how politics can get mixed up with the truth about what a follower of Jesus should really look like. Reading this book could be your newest opportunity for a spiritual upgrade as well.

Authority can also be a hard pill to swallow when you haven't had decent leadership role models in your life. However, Jeff uses Scripture to set the record straight and he shoots down all the "woe is me" excuses we have all used, at one time or another. Jeff also shares some practical reminders. As he puts it, "You will never have the authority to the degree you want, unless you submit to the degree He wants." There are some compelling truths that bring God-honoring conviction and shine light on some of the ways we undermine the authorities in our lives that God himself has established.

One moment of conviction for me after reading this book, was to be compelled to come to a complete stop at stop signs. Gasp! Drive like Jesus is in the vehicle. Wait! He is. The goal is not perfection, but improvement. It all comes down to choice. If you desire to honor God, then choose to honor the authorities He has put in your life. The return on investment is huge! I hope you get challenged as you read this book and come through on the other side, with a new level of freedom in Jesus. This book is a great opportunity to embrace God's heart and perspective on authority.

-Philip Pantana, Jr.

INTRODUCTION

One morning, about six years ago, I woke up from a night of sleep, and I heard the words, "The Authority of the People of God." I don't believe I had opened my eyes yet. As I shook off sleep, I said, "What?".

"The Authority of the People of God," came the reply.

"What about it?" I asked.

"That's the name of your first book," said the Voice.

With a sigh, I said, "Good morning to You, too, Lord."

Now, it's not that I don't believe in writing books, and it's not that I don't believe in doing what God wants you to do, it's just that sometimes you are not ready for certain tasks that the Lord assigns to you, especially first thing in the morning. It is probably better to say, you don't feel ready. But God speaks to us, and gives us our assignments, in His timing. So despite what we might feel, or even believe, He proceeds with His plan. Our job is to obey.

For me, I don't know why He would want me to write this book. Many prominent Christians, past and present, who are way more skilled and further along the Christian walk than I am, have written on authority. Maybe I'm going to share something they did not, some extra layer of the onion that has not been revealed until now. It is a humbling and sobering thing to believe that God would use me in this way, to contribute to the pool of thought on authority. I don't believe I have learned everything there is to know about authority. But I do believe that the Lord has given me some insight into the topic that is critical for the Church in this hour.

This book is only about two things: 1) the potential of our authority as believers and, 2) our need for submission and obedience. Authority is a good thing. No, it's a great thing. It's a necessary thing. And it affects every facet, of every life, every day, and we cannot afford to not understand it. When it comes to authority, like so many other things in the Scriptures, we cannot afford to have our own opinion about it. We must live in the place of His opinion about it because His opinion is the only opinion that counts. Using the Bible, I am going to try and reveal God's perspective about authority based on what He has given us through the divine inspiration of the Word.

I am going to say things in this book that will not be popular. Somewhere along the way, the Church has been poisoned by some attitude that we are not allowed to say anything that cuts. We have been fed the line that Jesus is sweet all the time and never says anything hard to us; and that, my friends, is a satanic lie. If you want to know what God thinks of sin, then take a look at the abuse He allowed His Son to endure for you and me before and during His execution. He hates sin and wants to eradicate it out of our lives to that degree. If we think that means He will not ever rebuke us, call us up higher, hold us to a standard of righteousness, tell us to stop whining, or tell us to quit making excuses, then we are wrong.

The reason we need to talk about rebellion is that it is everywhere. It's prevalent in us and it's prevalent in our society. And I am seeing both good and bad things come out of the

Church regarding this issue. As the Body of Christ, our understanding of authority and submission needs to be deeper. In many circles, the church is just lacking a real understanding of rebellion. And there are a couple of reasons I think this lack exists.

First, I think when the church speaks about authority and rebellion in general, there is this superficial, cerebral, acknowledgment about it. Most people say "yes, I understand that authority is good, and rebellion is bad", but I think that is where the acknowledgment stops. And what I don't see is a real comprehension of it by most people in the Church. I don't see the recognition by many people of their behavior or thought patterns and actions, as rebellious. It's as if they hear what is being taught, but then there is no thought put into working the ideas out in their mind in an introspective way by asking themselves, "Hey, am I rebellious?". Folks, we must ask ourselves that question!

People hear sermons on rebellion, and they automatically assign its relevance to things, people, and events "out there". They process the message of labeling things rebellious as being reserved for criminals and outrageous conduct, when it's the subtle thoughts in our hearts that are the real problem. So, I'm writing on this topic to address behaviors and attitudes in us, in our hearts, where the seat of the will is. When we hear the word rebellion, it's like a dirty word, and people go into self-defense mode like that word can't apply to me. Well, I hate to be the one to tell you, but it applies to you. It applies to me, too, so we're in this together.

Secondly, and closely related to the first reason, I don't think that most people understand the seriousness of rebellion.

Brothers and sisters, rebellion is a super-serious issue. I think that most people seek to classify rebellious acts first. Like, out and out rioting, that's rebellious activity, crime, that's rebellious activity, and not something I am going to participate in. But not following my boss' directions because I think I am smarter than he is, well that's not rebellious, that's okay, because if I'm smarter, my company is better, and more prosperous by doing things my way.

From the Lord's perspective, the rebellion in the attitude toward the boss is the same as the rebellion of the rioter in the street. We don't think about rebellion like that. In a situation like the boss scenario, a lot of Christians I know justify their behavior and explain it away, and that is my real concern. That is where the real deception of rebellion lies.

The enemy is good at what he does. He is very convincing, and the way he convinces people to justify themselves and their actions is staggering. What I find is, most justification of rebellion in the church has God as its reason. And that's the enemy's work, too. He gets us to excuse our behavior by invoking God, or freedom in God, into situations, and it's just deception. There is so much justification for our behavior and our attitude, that rebellion is overlooked with impunity, and I am afraid for that in my life and the lives of believers everywhere.

So, I write to flesh out the idea of rebellion, and then you have to use that knowledge to examine yourself. I can't examine you for you. I can give you feedback, sure, but ultimately, you have to be willing to cast the lens introspectively and ask yourself the tough question, "am I rebellious?".

Now let me save you a little time, because the default answer is yes, you are. On some level, we all are. I am. Even if it's a little, there is rebellion in me. Why? Because I'm human, and I'm in process, and so are you. So as long as we are in process, which, last time I looked, is until the day we die, we will have rebellion in us. As a pastor, I've had some conversations with some sweet, sweet, elderly folks who have followed the Lord their whole lives, and they still have a little rebellion in their hearts. So, we don't age out of this, we mature and refine our way out of it, and the only way we can do that is by God's grace, our submission, and our repentance. That's the only way.

And this may be the hardest truth to confront for all of us, that in our person, we are rebellious. Now obviously there is the felonious criminal level of rebellion, which most of us are not, but then there is the I-speed-every-time-I-drive-my-car rebellion; one we would never do, the other we practice daily, but it's all rebellion to God. I want to peel back the veneer on this a little bit, expose it for just how ugly it is, and hopefully, we will all get a little farther down the path together and look more like Jesus when we're done.

But it is also with great fear for the Church that I write. God is coming back for a bride without spot or wrinkle, and the Scripture says we are to make ourselves ready. Yet not only are most Christians I see not ready, but they are also making absolutely no effort to make themselves ready. They are expecting God to ride in on a white horse and tap them with a magic wand to make everything alright. It is fantasy. We are called to kill our flesh, discipline ourselves, serve and submit, and humble ourselves before an Almighty God. Where has the fear of the Lord gone? Unfortunately, because we have a low view of rebellion, we're not going anywhere in the authority realm. We are passively rebellious, and the enemy has convinced us *en masse* that that is good enough because there are more rebellious people all around us. That is self-justification, and it is a vital tool of the enemy in our lives.

You might be asking, is rebellion a big deal, and how does this relate to authority? Well, every Christian (almost every Christian) wants to see God move. They want to lay hands on people and see them healed. They want to be able to speak to the demonic and see them flee. They want to declare this and declare that in the power of God and watch it take place. They want the tangible presence of God to show up and wow them. They want to walk with God as Moses did. They cry out "show us Your glory!" and they have no idea what they are asking.

I am convinced that the reason the Lord does not show up is because of His mercy for us. If He showed up, many of us might drop dead because of the compromise, rebellion, and sin in our life, so because of His mercy, He stays away. Oh, I believe He wants to come, but He loves us more than that. He loves us to the point where He would rather wait and let us mature and make good choices, so we will survive His appearance.

And I am not talking about His Second Coming, because when that time comes, nothing will stop Him from coming. No, I am talking about us wanting revival, wanting Him to show up and be with us, wanting Him to visit us in a way we believe we want Him, and in a way that some people believe they are entitled to have Him.

I am here to tell you that if you want to walk in the authority and the power of the Kingdom of God, then it requires a crucifixion of rebellion in your life, absolute submission, and absolute obedience. You will never have authority to the degree you want unless you submit to the degree He wants. And God is waiting for those who will step up to take upon themselves the authority of the Kingdom, but only when they have taken the place of the servant. We cannot have one without the other.

This book is not for everyone; not that it would not be useful to everyone, but there will be some who cannot read and absorb what it has to say. This is not an "am I saved or not saved?" book. This is a "to what degree am I submitted?" book. Many people blinded by their own willful ambition will not be able to submit themselves to the ideas of this book, because they are too bound in deception to realize that although they are blood-bought, Bible-believing, faith-affirming Christians, they are utterly rebellious.

On the other hand, if you have a heart, a posture, and a desire to understand the principles of the Kingdom of our God, and you seek to be like Him as He is, read on; because this book is about His plan for you and me, collectively His people. We are purposed and destined for what is contained in these pages; not because this is my idea, but because this is His idea. I am not writing Scripture, but hopefully, I am illuminating what is already there by the wisdom and insight of the Holy Spirit. We can walk in the power and authority of God, to the same degree that Jesus did. There is no shortcoming on God's part in that offer. He is merely waiting to see who will accept it. I want to be one of those people who will, and I hope and pray that you do, too.

My prayer is that you will not be offended by what I've written, but if offense is what it takes to move you out of your stubbornness and rebellion, and into a place of obedience, then so be it. You'll be better for it in the end. May the God of all grace enable and equip you to read the words contained in these pages. May they change your life so that you can walk in the authority of the Kingdom of God and utterly rout the enemy and all his works!

1
GOD

In the beginning, God created the heavens and the earth.
-Genesis 1:1

In the beginning, God … . Wherever that was, whenever it was, the beginning was in God. It is fitting, therefore, that we start at the beginning. To understand authority, or any other topic, we must begin with God. Because it is God who creates, designs, and purposes everything.

This is why we are not entitled to our own opinion, about anything. God's viewpoint is the only viewpoint that matters. Many Christians would save themselves years of heartache, worry, and stress if they would just be willing to look at things from God's point of view. I have listened to Bill Johnson speak hundreds of times. He consistently says one thing that is a life lesson that we all need to ingest. He says, "I can't afford to have one thought about me that He (God) doesn't have about me." I agree emphatically. I would also add, we cannot afford to have one thought about anything that He doesn't have about anything.

God gives us our minds to think, create, ponder, and imitate our Father with, so I am not condemning free thought, analysis, or opinion. What I am saying is we must hold our opinions and conclusions loosely, because we are often wrong, but God never is. One of my biggest concerns for the Church is the health of her people. I want to see emotionally healthy and strong people in the Church, and what I see is a sea of emotionally unhealthy, wounded people. It is one of the reasons that I am passionate about healing—physical, spiritual, and emotional. One of the ways people stay in an unhealthy condition, instead of growing into maturity in the Lord, is by refusing, consciously or unconsciously, to have their minds renewed. They continue to think their thoughts, instead of God's thoughts. They insist on looking at things from their perspective, instead of His perspective, and they demand that He conform to their will, versus them conforming to His. God coming down to our level is just not going to happen. God is the immutable God. He will not change. He cannot change. He is unchangeable. And thank God that He is! Some people in the future are going to be very disappointed to see that God is going to do exactly what He has said He will do.

God is the Eternal One. He is the King of the Ages. He is the Almighty God and there is no other. He is everything good, righteous, and holy. There is none like Him in all of Creation, or outside of Creation. He stands alone in pre-history, history, and post-history. No one is His rival, nor is there anyone who can compete for His throne. He is unbeatable, unquenchable, and immovable. He is the great I AM. And we should marvel at the mention of His name. You might say that you have heard that before, but are you living in the reality of those statements? If you are, it has changed your life. If you are not, then you are plagued by all sorts of wrong thinking and circumstances, not the least of which is a low view of God. Read what the great

A.W. Tozer says from his book, *The Knowledge of the Holy,*

> What comes into our minds when we think about God is the most important thing about us. The history of mankind will probably show that no people has ever risen above its religion, and man's spiritual history will positively demonstrate that no religion has ever been greater than its idea of God. Worship is pure or base as the worshiper entertains high or low thoughts of God. For this reason the gravest question before the Church is always God Himself, and the most portentous fact about any man is not what he at a given time may say or do, but what he in his deep heart conceives God to be like. We tend by a secret law of the soul to move toward our mental image of God. This is true not only of the individual Christian, but of the company of Christians that composes the Church. Always the most revealing thing about the Church is her idea of God, just as her most significant message is what she says about Him or leaves unsaid, for her silence is often more eloquent than her speech. She can never escape the self-disclosure of her witness concerning God. Were we able to extract from any man a complete answer to the question, "What comes into your mind when you think about God?" we might predict with certainty the spiritual future of that man. Were we able to know exactly what our most influential religious leaders think of God today, we might be able with some precision to foretell where the Church will stand tomorrow.[1]

I would ask you to do one thing before you read on. Examine your viewpoint of God. From your perspective, is He good? Is He the great I AM? Is He the Lord God Almighty, or have you fashioned some image or perception of Him in your mind? Is He your Lord? Is He Master? Do you have a high view of God or a low view of God? If high, is it as high as it could be or is there room for improvement?

To think of God, other than what He is, is to commit idolatry. He does not have to conform to our opinion and that is not the point of this mental exercise. We have to conform to His. So the point of our examination is to see if, in any way, our thoughts of God are ignoble. If they are, I encourage you to have them corrected. Work through them, find out why they are the way they are and if they don't line up with what the Word of God says about Him, then put those thoughts to death. Repent and forgive God. Not because He did anything wrong, but because you entered into a wrong belief about Him and have held Him in contempt for things you think He was or did. It is only from a correct posture, that you have any hope of a right understanding of God, authority, and many other topics that influence your life.

2
SATAN

And He said to them, "I saw Satan fall like lightning from heaven."
-Luke 10:18

As much as I loathe the idea of writing a chapter about Satan, the comparison is necessary because Christians don't think rightly about Satan either. In short, there is no comparison between God and Satan. Satan is not the opposite of God, although his every quality is opposite of God's qualities. Satan is what is left when you remove God from something. He is not all-powerful, and he is not the other half of some cosmic contest. He is a created being that chose. If you did not ingest that last line, read it again. He chose things that he did not have the liberty to choose. He did not even choose, he just thought he would choose. He said in his heart that he would ascend and elevate his throne above God's. The Bible does not say that he did accomplish this, he merely thought it in his heart.

> How you are fallen from heaven, O Lucifer, son of the morning! *How* you are cut down to the ground, you who weakened the nations! For you have said in your heart: "I will ascend into heaven, I will exalt my throne above the stars of God; I will also sit on the mount of the congregation on the farthest sides

of the north; I will ascend above the heights of the clouds, I will be like the Most High."

-Isaiah 14:12-14

He was a created being with delegated authority because he had a throne to try and elevate. There is a takeaway here for us as believers. In his heart, Satan merely thought about usurping God's authority. What was the response from God? Satan fell like lightning from the sky, cut down to the ground. Have you seen the force with which lightning proceeds from the heavens? It is violent, and it is sudden. In an instant, for merely the thought, Satan was cast down in the same manner, with the same force, and the same violence that lightning comes forth. That should paint a clear picture for us of what God thinks about authority and how He responds to rebellion.

Contrary to popular belief, Satan did not organize a heavenly war. There's no indication that he assembled an army. No, he conceived a thought in his heart, and that thought decimated him for eternity. How many messages have you heard from the pulpit that talk about how sin begins as a thought sown in the mind? Is it any surprise that Satan would use that which resulted in his fall, to try and bring about your fall?

In response to that thought, God took action; swiftly, severely, and with violence. The response is clear, rebellion will not be tolerated; more, the *thought* of rebellion will not be tolerated. God is that serious about His authority. The consequences for Satan are unchangeable. No salvation can be afforded to him, and there is no hope for his future. He is damned, but that is not the same for you and me. Thank You, Lord, for Your mercy!

Sadly, in the same vein as Satan, we assault God's authority with seeming impunity, but I tell you, Christian, it is only seemingly. "Be not deceived; God is not mocked: for whatsoever a man soweth, that shall he also reap" (Galatians 6:7, KJV). God's grace alone, saves us from His response to our rebellion, but His response has only been temporarily stayed. There is coming a day when the fury and the righteous anger of the Lord will break forth upon the earth and its people in judgment. And the rebellion that is in the earth, and the hearts of its people will be dealt with like Satan was; suddenly, violently, and severely. Let us take heed to ourselves, lest we die.

3

THE AUTHORITY OF GOD

I am the Lord, and there is no other; There is no God besides Me. I will gird you,
though you have not known Me, that they may know from the rising of the sun to
its setting that there is none besides Me. I am the Lord, and there is no other; I
form the light and create darkness, I make peace and create calamity;
I, the Lord, do all these things.
-Isaiah 45:5-7

Authority is a big deal. In my life personally, authority is what I walk in every day. See, I am the husband of a wonderful wife and a father to four great kids. In that capacity, I am an authority in my household. I am also a pastor of a church and that brings with it a position of authority. I am responsible for other people's lives in my church, and even more importantly, the Scripture says that I will have to give an account for them on the day of judgment. Lastly, I also have a secular profession. I am a warden of a detention center. I've worked in the Corrections field since I was 19 years old. So, I became a man of authority at 19. Now, I did not know that then, and I certainly did not comprehend it to the degree that I do today, but I was in that role, nonetheless. Now 27 years later, authority has defined my life and God has used my experiences in the secular world to teach me about authority, and people, and how to manage issues of authority. But even with 27 years of a wide array of experience, I don't get to have an opinion about authority that does not line up with Scripture. Sure, I have learned a lot in the world. I have seen good authority and bad, but regardless of what was presented to me, or what I think, or how I have been treated or mistreated, I have to let the Bible define this issue for me, and every other issue in my life for that matter.

So, what does authority mean for the Christian? The first point I want to make is, authority is a primary principle of the Kingdom of God. Authority is every bit as important as holiness, salvation, and the resurrection of Jesus. And I will tell you why. It is a repeat of chapter one. It all started with Him. From God's lips, He has declared that He is the only God in existence. There is no other. He began everything. He created everything. It was by His authority that we were and are created. Indeed, He upholds everything by the word of His power (Hebrews 1:3).

There are two types of authority in existence, and only two. These are *intrinsic* authority and *delegated. Intrinsic* means "naturally belonging". Synonyms of intrinsic are "inherent" and "innate". God's authority is intrinsic. He is the only being in existence whose authority naturally belongs to Him. God has a legitimate right to His authority, both by His person, and position. He has authority by His person because He is God, and He has authority by His position because He is God.

This also means that authority is a primary principle of the Kingdom of God. It is a foundation stone. Authority begins and ends with God. Authority flows from His eternal throne, and there is nothing that surpasses the authority of God, or that overthrows it. God's authority is final, and it cannot be disputed. He is the one true God. We find this asserted in several passages of Scripture.

> I, even I, am the Lord, and besides Me there is no Savior.
>
> -Isaiah 43:11

> Thus says the Lord, the King of Israel, And his Redeemer, the Lord of hosts: "I am the First and I am the Last; Besides Me there is no God. And who can proclaim as I do? Then let him declare it and set it in order for Me, Since I appointed the ancient people. And the things that are coming and shall come, Let them show these to them. Don't fear, nor be afraid; Have I not told you from that time, and declared it? You are My witnesses. Is there a God besides Me? Indeed there is no other Rock; I know not one."
>
> -Isaiah 44:6-8

> I am the Lord, and there is no other; There is no God besides Me. I will gird you, though you have not known Me, that they may know from the rising of the sun to its setting, that there is none besides Me. I am the Lord, and there is no other; I form the light and create darkness, I make peace and create calamity; I, the Lord, do all these things. Rain down, you heavens, from above, And let the skies pour down righteousness; Let the earth open, let them bring forth salvation, And let righteousness spring up together. I, the Lord, have created it. Woe to him who strives with his Maker! Let the potsherd strive with the potsherds of the earth! Shall the clay say to him who forms it, "What are you making?" Or shall your handiwork say, "He has no hands?" Woe to him who says to his father, "What are you begetting?" Or to the woman, "What have you brought forth?" Thus says the Lord, The Holy One of Israel, and his Maker: "Ask Me of things to come concerning My sons;

And concerning the work of My hands, you command Me. I have made the earth, And created man on it. I—My hands—stretched out the heavens, And all their host I have commanded. I have raised him up in righteousness, And I will direct all his ways; He shall build My city and let My exiles go free, Not for price nor reward," Says the Lord of hosts. The Lord, the Only Savior, Thus says the Lord: "The labor of Egypt and merchandise of Cush And of the Sabeans, men of stature, Shall come over to you, and they shall be yours; They shall walk behind you, They shall come over in chains; And they shall bow down to you. They will make supplication to you, saying, 'Surely God is in you, And there is no other; There is no other God.'" Truly You are God, who hide Yourself, O God of Israel, the Savior! They shall be ashamed and also disgraced, all of them; They shall go in confusion together, Who are makers of idols. But Israel shall be saved by the Lord With an everlasting salvation; You shall not be ashamed or disgraced forever and ever. For thus says the Lord, Who created the heavens, Who is God, Who formed the earth and made it, Who has established it, Who did not create it in vain, Who formed it to be inhabited: I am the Lord, and there is no other. I have not spoken in secret, in a dark place of the earth; I did not say to the seed of Jacob, "Seek Me in vain;" I, the Lord, speak righteousness, I declare things that are right. Assemble yourselves and come; Draw near together, You who have escaped from the nations. They have no knowledge, Who carry the wood of their carved image, And pray to a god that cannot save. Tell and bring forth your case; Yes, let them take counsel together. Who has declared this from ancient time? Who has told it from that time? Have not I, the Lord? And there is no other God besides Me, A just God and a Savior; There is none besides Me. Look to Me, and be saved, All you ends of the earth! For I am God, and there is no other. I have sworn by Myself; The word has gone out of My mouth in righteousness, And shall not return, That to Me every knee shall bow, Every tongue shall take an oath. He shall say, "Surely in the Lord I have righteousness and strength. To Him men shall come, And all shall be ashamed who are incensed against Him. In the Lord all the descendants of Israel Shall be justified, and shall glory."

-Isaiah 45:5-25

With this latest set of verses, we see God declaring from His mouth, His authority, His right to reign, His right to make us, fashion us, and do whatever enters into His heart to do. He alone is justified in all of His actions and all of His ways. Who are we to question Him? When I hear the accusations of unbelievers and scoffers who question the motives and actions of God it makes me righteously angry. Who are they to question the Almighty God who makes the heavens and the earth?

There is nothing in existence that can question the authority of God. Every human being would be wise to settle this down in their hearts. This one principle alone, if acknowledged by every man, could change the world as we know it. But how great would the effect be in the earth if only the Church of Jesus believed this with all of their heart, all of their mind, and all of their strength? It would solve every issue of rebellion, striving, frustration, anxiety, fear, and complacency. It would also bring unending revival! Church, hear the Word of the Lord; He is God, and there is no other!!

4
THE AUTHORITY OF MAN

Then God said, "Let Us make man in Our image, according to Our likeness; let them have dominion over the fish of the sea, over the birds of the air, and over the cattle, over all the earth and over every creeping thing that creeps on the earth." So God created man in His own image; in the image of God He created him; male and female He created them. Then God blessed them, and God said to them, "Be fruitful and multiply; fill the earth and subdue it; have dominion over the fish of the sea, over the birds of the air, and over every living thing that moves on the earth."
-Genesis 1:26-28

The second type of authority is *delegated authority*. Since God alone is the only intrinsic authority in existence, every other authority that exists is delegated authority. *There is no other authority type.*

For delegated authorities, their authority does *not* naturally belong to them. They have received it either by who they are, or what position they have, but in either case, they have received it from God. Whether they know it, understand it, or acknowledge it is irrelevant. Let's use some basic examples. I am a parent. As a father, I have authority over my children. Where do I get that authority from? I get it from God. I received that authority from God because He gave me the ability to create children. If I did not have the capability as a human to create children, then I would not have authority in that capacity. Certainly, I can also be delegated this authority if I were in a position to adopt children as my own.

In my secular profession, I am a warden. Where do I get that authority? I get it from God. I received the authority from my employer, who is backed by the Federal government, who is backed by the three branches of government, which is backed by the Declaration of Independence, in which our sovereignty and independence as Americans were declared, as God-given inalienable rights. As a result, my authority as a warden is backed by earthly and godly authority. If I did not have authority, I could not do what I do. I would not be responsible or accountable for anyone or anything if I did not have the authority to do so. Without authority, I have no power. With authority, I have power equal to the level of my authority. These two types of authority, *intrinsic* and *delegated*, are the only two types of authority that exist, or that will ever exist. Anything or anyone that tries to claim authority without having genuine authority is simply counterfeit.

How did delegated authority begin on earth? Well, it began in the garden of Eden with God's original plan. We see in the first chapter of Genesis that God made Adam. Adam means "man, human being". So, God made an adam and called him Adam. And He set Adam in the garden to work it, tend to it, and exercise dominion over it. Right before that, God was the only authority in existence (in the human context. He may have delegated authority to the Heavenly host), but the moment that He made Adam, He delegated some measure of the authority of the Godhead to Adam. In short, He put Adam in charge. Then He commanded Adam to subdue the whole earth. He said, "Be fruitful and multiply; fill the earth and subdue it; have dominion over the fish of the sea, over the birds of the air, and over every living thing that moves on the earth" (Genesis 1:28). Something new had taken place. God, for the first time, had delegated His authority to another, to one of His earthly creations.

Genesis 2:15, "Then the Lord God took the man and put him in the garden of Eden to tend and keep it." In Hebrew, the word for the English word "keep" is *shamar*, and it means to keep, guard, observe, to watch over, to protect.[2] It is also the primary word for watchmen throughout the Old Testament. So, Adam was set on the earth, in the garden, to be God's watchman on the earth.

This mandate is confirmed in Psalm 8:

> O Lord, our Lord, How excellent is Your name in all the earth, Who have set Your glory above the heavens! Out of the mouth of babes and nursing infants You have ordained strength, Because of Your enemies, That You may silence the enemy and the avenger. When I consider Your heavens, the work of Your fingers, The moon and the stars, which You have ordained, What is man that You are mindful of him, And the son of man that You visit him? For You have made him a little lower than the angels, And You have crowned him with glory and honor. You have made him to have dominion over the works of Your hands; You have put all things under his feet, All sheep and oxen—Even the beasts of the field, The birds of the air, And the fish of the sea that pass through the paths of the seas. O Lord, our Lord, How excellent is Your name in all the earth!
>
> -Psalm 8:1-9

In verse 6, the English word *dominion* is translated from the Hebrew word, *mashal*, and it means to rule, to reign, or to have dominion over. It is clear from these passages that God's original plan was that man would be the delegated authority of God on the earth. It is only natural that His idea continues to permeate everything since. Just because the Fall happened, and man allowed sin into the equation, does not change the plan and purpose of God.

We need to understand then that by God-given right, everything on the face of the earth is subjected to us as humans. Nothing has been left out of the phrase "every living thing that moves on the earth". It is from here that we distinguish ourselves from the animal rights activist or the environmentalist that both exalt the earth and its creation above man. Neither the responsible management of animal life nor the stewardship of the planet should be ignored. They both have a rightful place; however, we cannot swing the pendulum to the other extreme to magnify either the animal or the earth above mankind. Neither is more important than the image-bearers of God. To do so is to leave the bounds of godly order and design and enter into sin. "You have made man a little lower than the angels," cried the Psalmist. We can rightly protect the earth, steward it and its creatures, and not abandon our position of authority over all of those things. We were created, therefore, to be image-bearers of God. We are to re-present Him in everything we do.

When Satan targeted Eve in the Garden, I am convinced that he was there to bring her into sin, but I am further convinced that he was after the authority that had been given to man. You will never convince me that Satan did not understand how the principles of authority worked. He was around long enough (however long that was) to observe how the Kingdom of God functioned. He had been given authority in heaven before his rebellion. We should not underestimate our adversary—and I don't mean to give honor to him in any way—but he is not ignorant of God, the Kingdom of God, or how the Kingdom operates. He targeted Eve because his primary objective was to steal the authority she carried, and he got it when she fell and when she caused her husband to fall.

To prove this, we need not look further than the temptation of Christ when Satan offered his authority to Jesus in exchange for worship.

> Then the devil, taking Him up on a high mountain, showed Him all the kingdoms of the world in a moment of time. And the devil said to Him, "All this authority I will give You, and their glory; for this has been delivered to me, and I give it to whomever I wish. Therefore, if You will worship before me, all will be Yours."
>
> -Luke 4:5-7

"For this has been delivered to me ..." as if the authority of man was wrapped up in a bow and presented to Satan when Adam fell. Notice Jesus did not refute the devil's claim about that authority. Jesus merely refused to take a shortcut to what was rightfully His. Thankfully the Lord knew His purpose and had His trust placed in the Father's plan. That which the devil obtained by deception, and offered, would soon be rent from his hands, delivered to the Lord, and restored to mankind.

5
REASONING

*"Come now, and let us reason together," Says the Lord,
"Though your sins are like scarlet, They shall be as white as snow;
Though they are red like crimson, They shall be as wool.
-Isaiah 1:18*

For the remainder of this book, the things we have to discuss are delegated authority as it pertains to authority in the earth, submission to authority and our responsibilities, rebellion, and the authority of the people of God. But before I get to those subjects, we must take a look at *reasoning*. There are tough and direct implications we must learn from the subjects that follow. For some, those implications will not be pleasant. If we look at delegated authority and the issues that surround it, and if we look at our authority as believers and followers of Christ, and we don't have our reasoning straight, we will be wasting our time, because we will immediately set ourselves to trying to reason why we should or should not obey delegated authority, and whether we do have or don't have authority as the people of God.

The ideas expressed in God's view of delegated authority and God's view of our authority are counter-cultural. In fact, in some circumstances, they are counter-religious. So, we have to make sure that our minds are renewed, having been washed with the water of the Word, so that we can rightly *reason* about these issues. God's Word is very clear on these matters, and thus we should be clear on these matters. But often we are not. We are not clear *because* of our poor reasoning. So hopefully, if we get our minds and reasoning right, we will be able to rightly position ourselves to understand authority better.

Reasoning is the use of reason; specifically, it is the drawing of inferences or conclusions through the use of reason. Reason is:

1. a statement offered in explanation or justification <gave reasons that were quite satisfactory>
2. a rational ground or motive <a good reason to act soon>
3. a sufficient ground of explanation or of logical defense; especially something (as a principle or law) that supports a conclusion or explains a fact <the reasons behind her client's action>
4. the thing that makes some fact intelligible: cause <the reason for earthquakes>
5. the power of comprehending, inferring, or thinking especially in orderly rational ways: intelligence
6. proper exercise of the mind
7. sanity
8. the sum of the intellectual powers[3]

So reasoning involves using this intellectual, intelligible process to think about, comprehend, explain, or give rationale to a topic. It is an activity of the mind or the intellect, but it is more than a cerebral process. Reason is not confined to our minds. At its core, reason is done at the level of the heart, at the seat of decision, in the will. We logically think through things, and we decide our responses to what we have thought about. What does this have to do with authority, you might be asking?

It has a lot to do with authority. Authority at its core has to do with the principles of rebellion or submission. There is no third option. We make decisions every day that tangibly demonstrate our propensity toward being obedient or being rebellious. Those decisions are the product of our thoughts, intents, and motives, in other words, our reasoning. So reasoning has everything to do with authority. If our reasoning tends towards rebellion, we will be rebellious. If our reasoning tends towards submission, we will be obedient. The problem, thus, is not our reasoning, but what we do with it. Reasoning is necessary, it is proper, and it is ordained of God. God does not expect robotic compliance or token obedience. We must obey because God is God and He commands it, but He desires that we cognitively obey.

Now let me say this, and I will expand on it more in just a minute. Our lack of understanding does not permit us to be disobedient. This is an excuse that I see far too many Christians use. "Well I don't understand, so I'm not…"; "Why should I (fill in the blank)?" As I said earlier, we must obey God because He is God, but He has designed us to know and understand why we must obey. In times when it is unclear why, we must trust in Him and His character and not look to ourselves to justify our disobedience based on ignorance.

We must obey because God is THE authority and He is inherently good; therefore, to obey God is ALWAYS a good thing, and good for us. And because He is good, He would never steer us wrongly or lead us to something evil. He is not against us knowing, He is not against intellect or knowledge, or understanding. Throughout the Scripture, He encourages wisdom. In fact, in Proverbs 1:7, the Bible says, "The fear of the Lord is the beginning of knowledge; fools despise wisdom and instruction." I would also argue that a lack of fear of the Lord is rebellious because if we recognized Him as THE authority it should invoke some reverence for Him.

Blessed is the one who finds wisdom, and the one who gets understanding.

-Proverbs 3:13

And now, O sons, listen to me: blessed are those who keep my ways. Hear instruction and be wise, and do not neglect it. Blessed is the one who listens to me, watching daily at my gates, waiting beside my doors. For whoever finds me finds life and obtains favor from the Lord, but he who fails to find me injures himself; all who hate me love death."

-Proverbs 8:32-36 (ESV)

Folly is a joy to him who lacks sense, but a man of understanding walks straight ahead.

-Proverbs 15:21 (ESV)

How much better to get wisdom than gold! To get understanding is to be chosen rather than silver.

-Proverbs 16:16

Whoever gets sense loves his own soul; he who keeps understanding will discover good.

-Proverbs 19:8

My son, eat honey, for it is good, and the drippings of the honeycomb are sweet to your taste. Know that wisdom is such to your soul; if you find it, there will be a future, and your hope will not be cut off.

-Proverbs 24:13-14

God is Wisdom and He has designed us to know Him. He has designed us to be wise. He advises us to live rightly and be wise. He says:

> Wash yourselves; make yourselves clean; remove the evil of your deeds from before my eyes; cease to do evil, learn to do good; seek justice, correct oppression; bring justice to the fatherless, plead the widow's cause. "Come now, let us reason together," says the Lord: though your sins are like scarlet, they shall be as white as snow; though they are red like crimson, they shall become like wool. If you are willing and obedient, you shall eat the good of the land; but if you refuse and rebel, you shall be eaten by the sword; for the mouth of the Lord has spoken.
>
> -Isaiah 1:16-20 (ESV)

Where reasoning goes wrong is where a man decides, within his intellect and reasoning, that he can reason aside from or apart from God. God is wisdom; therefore, there is no sound reasoning apart from Him.

How is man rebellious or obedient? Man is rebellious or obedient in thoughts, words, and actions. Thoughts, words, and actions come out of our reason. We reason and then we think, speak, or act. Sometimes we reason well, and sometimes we reason not so well. So, if reason is the root of thoughts, words, and actions, then we need to deal with our reasoning. If our reasoning is sound, biblical, and godly, then our thoughts, words, and actions will be sound, biblical, and godly. And I want to be clear here. I am not necessarily talking about always understanding everything. This reasoning will not always mean we know the reasons why to all of our questions. It also does not mean we are entitled to understand everything before we obey. No! Quite the opposite. In terms of submission, if the Lord gives us a direction to go or He gives us instruction, we are to do it. We are to be obedient and do what He asks us to do. In those moments, it may, or may not be for us to understand the reasons why. We are in no position to offer counsel to God, nor to try and comprehend His reasoning for things. A lot of the time we will not know why, we only need to do what we are asked. In Exodus 33, God says, "And I will be gracious to whom I will be gracious, and will show mercy on whom I will show mercy." So, it is His prerogative, and we are in no position to question. So, I am not talking about always "getting it" or understanding why God does what He does. What I am talking about is how we govern ourselves.

Man's reasoning first came into play in the Garden of Eden. Eve was the first person to employ reasoning.

> The Lord God took the man and put him in the garden of Eden to work it and keep it. And the Lord God commanded the man, saying, "You may surely eat of every tree of the garden, but of the tree of the knowledge of good and evil you shall not eat, for in the day that you eat of it you shall surely die."
>
> -Genesis 2:15-17

When Eve was tempted in the Garden, she added words to the instructions she had been given, which was not what God said. Let's read it.

> Now the serpent was more crafty than any other beast of the field that the Lord God had made. He said to the woman, "Did God actually say, 'You shall not eat of any tree in the garden'?" And the woman said to the serpent,

"We may eat of the fruit of the trees in the garden, but God said, 'You shall not eat of the fruit of the tree that is in the midst of the garden, neither shall you touch it, lest you die.'" *[God never said neither shall you touch it, lest you die.]* But the serpent said to the woman, "You will not surely die. For God knows that when you eat of it your eyes will be opened, and you will be like God, knowing good and evil." So when the woman saw that the tree was good for food, and that it was a delight to the eyes, and that the tree was to be desired to make one wise, she took of its fruit and ate, and she also gave some to her husband who was with her, and he ate. Then the eyes of both were opened, and they knew that they were naked. And they sewed fig leaves together and made themselves loincloths.

-Genesis 3:1-7

Now, she saw God every day in the Garden, and yet she failed to recognize Him as THE authority. Had she recognized God as the authority and recognized her husband as God's delegated authority, then the snake never would have been an issue. The snake was in no position to offer her counsel. However, the serpent introduced reasoning to her. "Did God really say?" By adding to what God said, she demonstrated that she did not know authority.

Let's use a diplomat as an example. A diplomat, or a representative of a ruling leader, conducts business on the behalf of the leader they represent. They need fully understand their position as a diplomat and what the boundaries of their authority are. **They cannot add to the guidance and instruction of the leader they represent if they feel like it**. They are to accurately and faithfully represent the leader who has appointed them. And if another voice challenges the ruler they represent, how long would a diplomat who negotiates with this competing voice keep their job? Probably not very long.

Eve did not understand authority. She carelessly added words to God's instructions, she then saw that the tree was good for food, and that it was a delight to the eyes, and that the tree was to be desired to make one wise, so she took of its fruit and ate, and she also gave some to her husband who was with her, and he ate. Eve sets about to reasoning. She looks at it, she listens to the serpent saying that it will make her wise, she reasons about all of those things, and poof, here we are. And faulty reasoning has never stopped. Ham reasoned that it would be funny to dishonor his father by uncovering his father's nakedness to his brothers, and it brought about a curse on his descendants. Miriam and Aaron reasoned themselves to be just as good a leader as Moses, and God reacted to their rebellion. Korah and company reasoned that they were just as elect as Moses, and God opened up the earth and swallowed them. Nadab and Abihu reasoned that they would offer sacrifices just any old way, and the fire of God consumed them. Saul reasoned it best to spare the Amalekites and to take it upon himself to offer sacrifices to God, and he lost the kingdom. David reasoned it was a good idea to have the ark of the covenant carried back to Jerusalem from the house of Abinadab on a new cart, and it cost Uzzah his life. And on and on we go through the Bible with example after example of mankind's reasoning.

So how do we reason properly? Should we reason at all? Yes, we should reason. We are to get rid of reasoning when it is negative, and we should utilize it when it is positive. How do we do this? The answer is found in 2 Corinthians 10:

"For though we walk in the flesh, we don't war according to the flesh. For the weapons of our warfare are not carnal but mighty in God for pulling down strongholds, casting down arguments and every high thing that exalts itself against the knowledge of God, bringing every thought into captivity to the obedience of Christ, and being ready to punish all disobedience when your obedience is fulfilled."

-2 Corinthians 10:3-6

We are to take every thought captive to obey Christ. As I reason, if my reasoning brings me into greater obedience with Christ, I am to employ it. If it brings me into contradiction with Christ, I am to cast it down and destroy it. I cannot trust it, and I cannot blindly reason. I need to examine everything I do and everything I say. I am never to assume that my reasoning is correct because my heart is evil and desperately wicked. My only insurance against myself is God in me, who makes me a new creation and a new creature in Christ. The One who renews my heart and mind with His Word. Thank You, Lord!

6
THE FALL

How you are fallen from heaven, O Lucifer, son of the morning!
-Isaiah 14:12

If we examine the world around us, the culture, the community we are each a part of, we will see an outworking of the result of sin and rebellion. Sin did not get Satan kicked out of heaven. Rebellion got Satan kicked out of heaven. Ambition came first, then rebellious thoughts in his heart, and sin was the result. Satan was submitted to and under the authority of God. I might add that he is still under the authority of God, but he is not submitted; he is in a permanent state of rebellion. Isaiah 14 tells us of his rebellion. It reads,

> How you are fallen from heaven, O Lucifer, son of the morning! How you are cut down to the ground, You who weakened the nations! For you have said in your heart: "I will ascend into heaven, I will exalt my throne above the stars of God; I will also sit on the mount of the congregation. On the farthest sides of the north; I will ascend above the heights of the clouds, I will be like the Most High."
>
> -Isaiah 14:12-14

Now, in context, this prophecy in Isaiah is about an earthly Babylonian king, so how do we get an inference about Satan? Is it proper biblical interpretation to infer meaning to the devil from this passage? It is proper, and I'll explain how, because it's not as plain as a reading of the text. So let me give a little hermeneutical sidebar. The KJV of Isaiah 14:12 says, "How art thou fallen from heaven, O Lucifer, son of the morning!" So, people read that and say, it says Lucifer, so the passage is talking about the devil. Why would the passage say Lucifer if it wasn't talking about the devil? Well, here's what happened. The KJV translators used the word Lucifer because they were translating from the Vulgate, and *Lucifer* is the word in this passage in the Vulgate. The Vulgate, as you may or may not know, was the Latin translation of the Bible written by Jerome in the 4th century. In Latin though, *Lucifer* is not a proper name. The KJV translators did not know what Lucifer meant when they came across it. So, they didn't try and interpret it, they just copied it straight from the Latin language to the English language. Because they did this, the word *Lucifer* since that time has been attributed as another name for the devil. The Bible never names Satan *Lucifer*; it's only been because of the translation of this passage that he has become known as Lucifer. *Satan* is not even a proper name. *Satan* should be translated as "the satan", or *the accuser*. *Lucifer* is the Latin word for "morning star" and the phrase *morning star* in Latin means *Venus*. But because of the actions taken by the KJV translators, people today say one of the devil's names is *Lucifer*, and it's also why there are about seven translations of the Bible that say *Lucifer*, and others say *morning star* or *day star*. So, does that create a problem for us, or can we still attribute this passage to the devil? Well, we can, but not because the word *Lucifer* is used. We can attribute it because of other passages in the Bible that give us revelation about Satan. So, is there a problem with the Isaiah passage referring to both a Babylonian king and Satan simultaneously? No, there is not. While it is primarily about an earthly Babylonian king, it's also a metaphorical passage to illustrate what happened with Satan. We see the same thing in Ezekiel 28. In that chapter, there is a prophecy against the Prince of Tyre. Let's look at it.

The word of the Lord came to me again, saying, "Son of man, say to the prince of Tyre, 'Thus says the Lord God: "Because your heart is lifted up, And you say, 'I am a god, I sit in the seat of gods, In the midst of the seas,' Yet you are a man, and not a god, Though you set your heart as the heart of a god (Behold, you are wiser than Daniel! There is no secret that can be hidden from you! With your wisdom and your understanding You have gained riches for yourself, And gathered gold and silver into your treasuries; By your great wisdom in trade you have increased your riches, And your heart is lifted up because of your riches)," 'Therefore thus says the Lord God: "Because you have set your heart as the heart of a god, Behold, therefore, I will bring strangers against you, The most terrible of the nations; And they shall draw their swords against the beauty of your wisdom, And defile your splendor. They shall throw you down into the Pit, And you shall die the death of the slain In the midst of the seas. "Will you still say before him who slays you, 'I am a god'? But you shall be a man, and not a god, In the hand of him who slays you. You shall die the death of the uncircumcised By the hand of aliens; For I have spoken," says the Lord God.'" Moreover the word of the Lord came to me, saying, "Son of man, take up a lamentation for the king of Tyre, and say to him, 'Thus says the Lord God: "You were the seal of perfection, Full of wisdom and perfect in beauty. You were in Eden, the garden of God; Every precious stone was your covering: The sardius, topaz, and diamond, Beryl, onyx, and jasper, Sapphire, turquoise, and emerald with gold. The workmanship of your timbrels and pipes Was prepared for you on the day you were created. "You were the anointed cherub who covers; I established you; You were on the holy mountain of God; You walked back and forth in the midst of fiery stones. You were perfect in your ways from the day you were created, Till iniquity was found in you. By the abundance of your trading You became filled with violence within, And you sinned; Therefore I cast you as a profane thing Out of the mountain of God; And I destroyed you, O covering cherub, From the midst of the fiery stones. "Your heart was lifted up because of your beauty; You corrupted your wisdom for the sake of your splendor; I cast you to the ground, I laid you before kings, That they might gaze at you."

-Ezekiel 28:1-17

This passage is an indictment and an announcement of punishment against the king of Tyre. We should not think the passage to be referring to two different people simply because verse 1 says *prince* and verse 12 says *king*. In Hebrew, the word translated *prince* is often translated as *ruler*. Therefore, verse 2 can be read in English, "Son of man, say to the ruler of Tyre…" So this is the same person, but we know that the man who was the king of Tyre was not a guardian cherub, we know he was not living on the mountain of God, and we know he wasn't in the garden of Eden. The king of Tyre at this point was Ethbaal II. So just like in Isaiah, the verses we see here for this earthly king are used metaphorically to describe what happened with Satan.

Now because of Eve, our authority as God's representation in the earth was lost. Adam and Eve handed their keys of authority to the devil, and he gladly took them. It was only the grace and mercy of God that restrained him for our sakes. It was also through the coming of Jesus that authority was restored to its rightful place. (I can't imagine living in a world where Satan had the right to authority and dominion in the earth.) Jesus' victory was complete, and we are made complete in Him, but we still have to deal with the fallout of the Fall in mankind. The consummation of the Kingdom is both now and not yet. As we move forward in time, towards the end of time, we will see the full outworking of sin and rebellion in the world around us. They will reach their climax before all things are settled once and for all and everything is brought into the subjection of the Lordship of Christ. When the authority of God was temporarily lost to Satan, rebellion set in. And it is to that topic that we turn our attention next.

7
REBELLION

For rebellion is as the sin of witchcraft,
and stubbornness is as iniquity and idolatry.
-1 Samuel 15:23

The French Philosopher Charles Baudelaire is often credited with the statement, "The greatest trick the devil ever pulled was convincing the world he didn't exist." I would submit to you that the second greatest trick the devil ever pulled is convincing the world and the church that rebellion is no big deal; that rebellion is a right we have whenever we don't agree with something; that we are justified in judging our leaders when we think they are wrong, and therefore we must rebel and disobey, or that we receive some sort of pass or exception to submitting and obeying them. And I can tell you definitively, that is not at all what the Bible teaches. The idea of rebellion is *satanic* and that's why we must be concerned with whether or not we are being rebellious.

Christian, we need not look further than some of the stories of Israel—in particular, the debacles of the children of Israel in the wilderness and later of King Saul—to see how the Lord feels about rebellion. In this chapter, I hope to make the case to you just how serious rebellion is in the eyes of the Lord, and maybe more importantly, WHY it is so serious.

Let's start with some definitions. The first Hebrew word for rebellion is *mᵊrî* (mer-ee'), it means *rebellion* or *rebellious*. It is found 23 times in the Old Testament. It is translated as rebellious (17x), rebellion (4x), rebel (1x), and bitter (1x). This word *mᵊrî* comes from the root of another Hebrew word *mârâh* (maw-raw'). Marah is used 44 times in the Old Testament and it is translated rebel (19x), rebellious (9x), provoke (7x), disobedient (2x), against (1x), bitter (1x), changed (1x), disobeyed (1x), grievously (1x), provocation (1x), and rebels (1x). The meaning is much broader with *mârâh*. It means to be contentious, be rebellious, be refractory, be disobedient towards, be rebellious against, (Qal) to be disobedient, to be rebellious towards father and to be disobedient, to be rebellious towards God, (Hiphil) to show rebelliousness, to show disobedience, to disobey.

Extra-biblical definitions of *rebellion* include armed resistance to an established government or ruler, defiance of authority or control, showing a desire to rebel, engagement in rebellion, difficult to control, unmanageable.

Now, these definitions are helpful and unhelpful at the same time. They are helpful in that they convey the seriousness of rebellion or rebellious activity. Provocation, rebel, provoke, disobedient—those are strong words. Even rebellion and rebellious are strong words. And so, they convey this idea of seriousness. Now they're unhelpful in that most Christians look at them and say, "well, I'm not a rebel," "I'm not disobedient," "I'm not rebellious." When in reality, that's exactly what we are. And so that is part of where the disconnect is. These are not labels we are going to place on ourselves normally or willingly, because we tend to believe those labels are reserved for criminals, gang members, general ruffians of society, "bad people", unbelievers, but certainly not Christians, and certainly not me. When in fact, these labels do apply to us if we are honest with ourselves.

I can tell you without reservation that we are off if we do not believe these labels ever apply to us, or if that's the way we dismiss these terms, that they don't apply. How do I know? Well, I know mostly because I know myself. I take matters of authority more seriously than most people I know. And even in myself I see rebellion. So if I can call myself rebellious, then most other people can call themselves rebellious, too. I find what distinguishes one rebel from another is the degree to which they submit when confronted with their rebellion. See some people tend towards submission and some tend towards rebellion.

When confronted with rebellion, people either a) stiffen or b) submit. Those are the only two options. I'm firmly in category B, and I hope that you are, too. When I'm confronted about rebellion by the Lord or by someone else, I submit. I'm almost always questioning myself and my posture, because I want to be sure to remain in a posture of submission more often than I want to remain in a posture of rebellion. I don't want to rebel, but it happens sometimes.

Some people I know wear rebellion as a badge of honor. I know a 60-something-year-old man, who is in ministry, who quite proudly told me he was a rebel in the Kingdom and that was his claim to fame. So, this is the first point. Rebellion is serious and it is in all of us, whether we think so or not. It's not cute, it's not funny, and it's not something to be proud of or boast about. We will be successful in the Kingdom of God only to the degree to which we are willing to take an honest look at ourselves and weigh our attitudes, thoughts, and actions in terms of our rebellion, and then submit. If we believe we are going to be spiritually great in the Kingdom while rebellious, we are never going to make it. And I mean never. I don't care what our ministry platform is or what kind of gifting we have, or which level of Christian ministry the Lord has allowed us to achieve by His grace thus far.

The Bible reveals a consistent, horrible, response from God to rebellion. If we want to see what God's response is, we just need to read the book of Numbers. In situation after situation in the wilderness, the Lord responded *violently* to rebellion in His people—not the world, **His people**. There are five instances of rebellion in Numbers, and when God responded to the rebellion, He responded with fury and wrath, and people died by the thousands in very extreme, painful ways. We're going to review these cases. And in reviewing them, I'm not trying to paint any sort of picture of something that can happen to us; rather, I'm simply trying to show what qualifies as rebellion in God's eyes, that we would never classify as rebellion in our own eyes, and how serious God is about it based on His reaction to it, because He never changes.

In Numbers 10, the people of God have just set out from Mount Sinai. They have gone through a census. The Lord has given instructions about Aaron and the Levites, the Tabernacle has been established, the pillar of cloud and fire is present. Things are getting started for real, and this is about two years *after* they've left Egypt. Think about that. They've been out of Egypt two years, and God is just now getting around to ordering them, organizing them, cleansing them, blessing them, telling them how to worship, and settling who is going to be responsible for what. Some people I know would not have made it that long. They would have been murmuring and complaining about how long it was taking to do anything or get anywhere. But they get some order to the gaggle as it were, and they set out from Mount Sinai. As soon as they set out, this happens:

> Now when the people complained, it displeased the Lord; for the Lord heard it, and His anger was aroused. So the fire of the Lord burned among them, and consumed some in the outskirts of the camp.
>
> -Numbers 11:1

We are not told what the cause of their complaining was. In Chapter 10, the last thing the Lord had told them to do was make these silver trumpets that will be used for various things, and other than that, they pack up the camp and move out. So, this is interesting to me. They complain—about what, we don't know—and the fire of the Lord consumed some people. Now, think about this; up until this point, the fire of the Lord has been an indicator of His presence with them, right? They had the pillar of fire, a tangible demonstration that God was there among them, and at this moment, that same comfort now becomes an affliction, because some of them did not survive His presence. Some of them were killed by it. The same Presence that brought comfort also dealt with sin.

Now let's stop right there. What was their sin? Their sin was complaining (which was a masquerade for unbelief). See, I told you, we're not talking about behavior that would be a crime.

They complained. Now we may read that story and have a hard time understanding why that was such a big deal. Did it warrant a judgment of instant death of being consumed by fire? Some might say no, it did not warrant death, after all, they were just complaining. But apparently, it did warrant death from God's perspective, because that is the sentence the Lord meted out. And since the Lord is unendingly good and just, apparently His justice in this situation was warranted, and it called for a stiff penalty. Do yourself a favor, always adopt the Lord's perspective, even if you don't understand it. At the end of the day, they complained against the Lord because they did not believe He would care for them. And that was an insult to the Lord and His character, and it was an accusatory act, and who is the *accuser*? The father of rebellion, that's who. And what is unfathomable to me, is these people had just come out of Egypt. They saw that in each plague, the plague affected only the Egyptians and the Israelites were protected. They saw the Red Sea part, and they walked through the middle of it, on dry ground! They witnessed with their own eyes the destruction of the Egyptians. How much more does one need to see before they will believe? So, this was an egregious sin in the eyes of the Lord. What they were shouting to God with their complaining was "We do not trust You!".

Also, observe that witnessing the supernatural was not enough to change their hearts or give them faith in God. Some Christians I know view the supernatural as the be-all-end-all solution to their unbelief. "If I could just see a miracle." Well, take it from the Israelites, they saw miraculous acts and wonders on a scale most of us never will, and in the end, it profited them nothing. Some of them still died in unbelief.

Now you would think seeing several of their traveling companions burn to death instantly would adjust the attitude of those that remained, but it did not. In the very next verse, after the fire is extinguished because of the intercession of Moses, they complain again, this time about having no meat to eat.

The Lord and Moses hear their complaining and both get angry. Moses wants to quit at this point, and he laments to the Lord about having to deal with these people by himself. The Lord appoints seventy elders of Israel to help him and promises to provide meat because of the people's complaints. But the Lord is going to provide so much meat that it is going to come out of their nose! The Lord fulfills His word to Moses and sends quail on the camp. But for those who complained, it would be their last meal. Verses 33 to 34 record their fate:

> But while the meat was still between their teeth, before it was chewed, the wrath of the Lord was aroused against the people, and the Lord struck the people with a very great plague. So he called the name of that place Kibroth Hattaavah, because there they buried the people who had yielded to craving.
>
> -Numbers 11:33-34

So here are two back-to-back issues of rebellion in the camp. One happens right after the other. No sooner have the corpses quit burning, than the complaining begins again, and the plague of the Lord starts wiping people out. And we know they died there because verse 34 says they buried them there. What a glaring message to the people of Israel: God is not to be rejected, complaining is not tolerated, ungratefulness and unbelief are met with death.

Personally, if I'm in this situation, I'm going low and figuring out how not to incur the wrath of God, and I'm doing so very, very expeditiously. But that's not what happens. In the very next chapter, Miriam and Aaron start discussing how they should be the boss. I guess we can't blame them, right? I mean in the first few days since leaving Mount Sinai this has been a colossal failure. People are dying left and right. So, Miriam and Aaron know the answer to the problem. It's time for a leadership change. What these people need is a new head coach. Aaron and Miriam are just as called, and just as anointed, and probably more so, because they are older and wiser than baby brother Moses, and they know better. If not outright leadership change, at least leadership by committee. More of a consensus type of leadership, where everyone has a voice, and we make decisions as a group. It sounds like an amazing development opportunity.

This is what they ask in Numbers 12:2, "Has the Lord indeed spoken only through Moses? Has He not spoken through us also?". And then five very sobering words of Scripture are recorded, "And the Lord heard it." The Lord calls out Moses, Aaron, and Miriam to the tent of meeting for a comeuppance of sovereign proportions. The Lord smites Miriam with leprosy from head to foot. What was her sin? Was it that she questioned God's delegated authority and elevated herself—no, she **vocalized thoughts** of elevating herself and her brother to a position of authority that was not hers to take—and the Lord heard it. If it were not for Moses' intercession, she would have died a leper, outside of the community of the people of God due to her rebellion. And these are the kind of stories we gloss over because we all know or have known Christians in today's day and age that have talked dismissively about their pastors or made similar comments that everyone in the Body of Christ can be used to lead. But these stories are here to show us how God thinks about these kinds of issues, and instead of taking away a good lesson on authority from the story, we gloss over or outright ignore the lessons of the story and then feign ignorance. But the truth is, we're without excuse.

Notice what Miriam said. Has the Lord indeed only spoken through Moses? Has He not spoken through us also? Now, let's think about this. What was wrong with that? Two simple questions. Has the Lord spoken only through Moses? The answer is no, the Lord hadn't only spoken through Moses. Has He not spoken through us also? Yes, He had spoken through them as well. God had spoken through her because Miriam was referred to as a prophetess. Exodus 15:20 calls Miriam, "Miriam the Prophet, Aaron's sister", so the Bible attests to the fact she was a prophet, which affirms that God has spoken through her. So, she's not asking questions that are out of bounds to ask.

So, what was the sin? The sin was the heart motive behind the question. The motive was a usurping of Moses' position and calling. Behind the motive was an elevation of herself and her brother Aaron. "The reflections of the heart belong to man, but the answer of the tongue is from the Lord. All a man's ways seem right to him, but the Lord evaluates the motives." (Proverbs 16:1-2 HCSB) It was the thought and intent of the heart that was revealed by Miriam's mouth, and what she said, that the Lord responded to. Give people enough time, and eventually, their mouths will reveal what is in their hearts. That should not surprise us. Out of the abundance of the heart the mouth speaks, the Bible says (Matthew 12:34).

Just by asking the question, Miriam was in rebellion. Not rioting, not violence, not breaking the law ... rebellion ... just ... speaking ... words ... revealing her corrupt heart ... rebellion. And look at the penalty! Leprosy! Ex-communication from the community would have been the permanent result if it weren't for Moses interceding for her.

To me, this story illustrates again the seriousness with which God treats authority and rebellion issues. If we think about it, this story is the same thing that Satan did to God when he was in heaven. He thought in his heart, "I will elevate my throne above the throne of God". There was the thought of usurping God, the ultimate Authority, and here, Miriam is doing the same thing, usurping in her heart God's delegated authority. So, these issues hit home for God. The other thing it illustrates is the subtleness of rebellion. She did not ask questions unreasonable to ask. Rebellion is sneaky, it is deceptive, it is blinding. It is extremely dangerous. And if we entertain it, things go very badly.

The next event we see comes from Numbers chapter 14. Let me set the stage for what is happening. In Chapter 13, the twelve spies of Israel have gone into the Promised Land. They've returned with a bad report, talking about how the land is filled with giants, and they spread fear about the situation throughout the people of God. So, in essence, the spies are more concerned with what they see as their circumstances in the natural, versus what God has said was going to happen.

And let's not dismiss the fact that acquiring the Promise Land was going to take work on their part. Sure, the Lord had

promised it to them, but that did not mean they were going to waltz into it and set up their houses. They were going to have to *war* for the promise to obtain it. A mistake that I often see Christians making is at the first sign of adversity in a matter, they give up, and that's not the proper response. When God says this or that is going to happen, then we rely on what He said, and we stand firm in what He has said, regardless of what it looks like in the natural, even if it means we go to war to get it.

So, they've received this report, and this is the people's response:

> So all the congregation lifted up their voices and cried, and the people wept that night. And all the children of Israel complained against Moses and Aaron, and the whole congregation said to them, "If only we had died in the land of Egypt! Or if only we had died in this wilderness! Why has the Lord brought us to this land to fall by the sword, that our wives and children should become victims? Would it not be better for us to return to Egypt?" So they said to one another, "Let us select a leader and return to Egypt."
>
> -Numbers 14:1-4

Are we seeing a pattern yet? Now, instead of just complaining, the people of Israel decide to double down and commit the sin of Miriam, and complain against their leadership, and they start fearing for their lives. Now they are ungrateful for their deliverance and are deceived into believing that what they had before in bondage was better than what God was offering to them for their future.

This should not shock us. We see this in the lives of

believers today. They want to stay in their Egypt. They long for the days of their bondage versus the freedom that God offers. It's deception, plain and simple, and this situation in Numbers is still common to the people of God. This brings us to the next point of rebellion. When rebellion begins, especially in a group of people, the best thing we can do is avoid the situation and the people perpetuating it. Why? Because **rebellion is contagious**.

Ten of the 12 spies bring a bad report. This bad report sows discord and fear in the hearts of others and the people come into agreement with it. Joshua and Caleb are not okay with the behavior of their friends and neighbors. They plead with the people not to say such things and they remind the people of what the Lord has done for them. Joshua and Caleb remained loyal to the Lord despite everyone around them turning their back on the Lord and the true leaders of Israel.

But it's to no avail. The dissatisfaction of these 10 spies spreads through the company of people like a disease. If we think the flu is contagious, it has nothing on rebellion. Next thing we know, the glory of the Lord lights up the Tabernacle. I have to say that in these instances, it's not a good sign when the glory of the Lord lights up the Tabernacle due to dissension and complaining. Instead of being excited at His appearance, they should be very, very concerned, because this is not going to end well. We're starting to see a negative pattern and the severe implications of having God's presence among you. Again, the Lord responds to their rebellion:

> Then the Lord said to Moses: "How long will these people reject Me? And how long will they not believe Me, with all the signs which I have performed among them? I will strike them with the pestilence and

disinherit them, and I will make of you a nation greater and mightier than they."

-Numbers 14:11-12

So again, we see the Lord's response to the rebellion, He is standing by ready to wipe them out for their complaining and unbelief. Like I said earlier, they weren't committing crimes, they weren't engaged in violence, this was a heart condition, and they were failing to see how serious it was.

Again, Moses intercedes for the people and the Lord relents. But the judgment for the people is still severe! So while intercession is made, and they are not immediately wiped out, there is still a severe penalty for them. No one alive over the age of twenty will get to see the Promised Land. They will all die in the wilderness. Let's read what the Lord says:

> Then the LORD said: "I have pardoned, according to your word; but truly, as I live, all the earth shall be filled with the glory of the LORD—because all these men who have seen My glory and the signs which I did in Egypt and in the wilderness, and have put Me to the test now these ten times, and have not heeded My voice, they certainly shall not see the land of which I swore to their fathers, nor shall any of those who rejected Me see it.
>
> "But My servant Caleb, because he has a different spirit in him and has followed Me fully, I will bring into the land where he went, and his descendants shall inherit it. Now the Amalekites and the Canaanites dwell in the valley; tomorrow turn and move out into the wilderness by the Way of the Red Sea."

-Numbers 14:20-25

Notice how verse 21 is one of our quotables? As Christians, we love declaring "all the earth shall be filled with the glory of the Lord." I love it, too, but we rarely hear people giving the context. The context is, the Lord is going to reveal His glory because He's going to bring about the death of those that did not put their faith in Him, those that rejected Him, and those that tested His patience. Yikes! And so, the penalty for this incident is that no one with the current group is going to make it to the Promised Land but Joshua and Caleb.

Next point about rebellion: **when you partner with rebellion, you can lose your inheritance**. Remember that, let me say it again, when you partner with rebellion, you can lose your inheritance. The whole generation of Israelites is infected with rebellion, it has spread like cancer, and it's enough to make God cut off the entire group from their inheritance. That's the danger of tolerating rebellion in your midst, trying to pacify it, trying to see things from their perspective, and sympathizing with rebellious people.

God is looking for loyalty. He wants loyal people who will believe Him, and not what things look like, and what other people try and pour in your ear. He wants you to believe in Him, over and above every other single thing. We have to remember that this was a community of God's people. God wants His people to live in community, but once we get to the point where we side more with the crowd, versus siding with the Lord, we've made the wrong choice. When we stand with people in their disagreement versus standing with the Lord and what He represents, we run the risk of being cut off. We have to put the Lord first in all things, and if we lose a relationship with others because we're following the Lord and what He says, we've made the right choice. I know that's tough to read, and that doesn't make it any easier, but the Lord does honor it.

And we see that in Joshua and Caleb. They choose to honor the Lord and what He said, and they are the only two who make it out of several million people. Think about that. Several million people get cut off and two survive. They would go on to lose every single person that they called their friends. Every single one. But in the end, they had the Lord and they had their inheritance. We have to choose wisely.

It bothers me today when I see Christians choosing earthly relationships over honoring the Lord. That's not right. So, when we're tempted to think that we're alone, or maybe we've gotten it wrong because we are in the minority, take heart, and remember Joshua and Caleb. Let's read the sad ending to this particular occasion.

And the LORD spoke to Moses and Aaron, saying, "How long shall I bear with this evil congregation who complain against Me? I have heard the complaints which the children of Israel make against Me. Say to them, 'As I live,' says the LORD, 'just as you have spoken in My hearing, so I will do to you: The carcasses of you who have complained against Me shall fall in this wilderness, all of you who were numbered, according to your entire number, from twenty years old and above. Except for Caleb the son of Jephunneh and Joshua the son of Nun, you shall by no means enter the land which I swore I would make you dwell in. But your little ones, whom you said would be victims, I will bring in, and they shall know the land which you have despised. But as for you, your carcasses shall fall in this wilderness. And your sons shall be shepherds in the wilderness forty years, and bear the brunt of your infidelity, until your carcasses are consumed in the wilderness. According to the number of the days in which you spied out the land, forty days, for each day you shall bear your guilt one year, namely forty years, and you shall know My rejection. I the LORD have spoken this. I will surely do so to all this evil congregation who are gathered together against Me. In this wilderness they shall be consumed, and there they shall die."" Now the men whom Moses sent to spy out the land, who returned and made all the congregation complain against him by bringing a bad report of the land, those very men who brought the evil report about the land, died by the plague before the LORD.

-Numbers 14:26-37

Verse 34 is very scary to me. These are God's people, but the ramification of their choices is, they shall know the Lord's rejection. I don't ever want to know the Lord's rejection. And He still feeds them; He still makes sure their clothes and their sandals don't wear out; He still protects them from their enemies; He is still faithful to them despite their unfaithfulness, but they are the walking dead. They are rejected, without hope, and there is nothing they can do to earn back their inheritance. The judgment on the men who encouraged rebellion is more instantaneous. They are brought before the Lord, and they die instantly of plague. Again, a tangible sign of how seriously the Lord treats rebellion.

After this, unfortunately, rebellion continues to be a persistent theme in Israel. The next group of people to be affected is the leadership. Rebellion has taken root in the camp, and the leaders are not exempt from it. We're not told this, but I bet the people who were rebellious just kept talking, and kept discussing it, and kept bringing it up. I don't think these leaders would have fallen if it weren't for that. If they would have, I don't believe they would have been made leaders to begin with. But the constant murmuring, and complaining, and talking probably wore them down.

In Numbers 16, Korah, Dathan, and Abiram raise up a crowd of 250 leaders to question the leadership of Moses and Aaron. Like Miriam, they propose to elevate themselves from their current positions of leadership to higher levels of leadership, and in so doing align themselves against who God has chosen to lead. Let's read what happens.

> Now Korah the son of Izhar, the son of Kohath, the son of Levi, with Dathan and Abiram the sons of Eliab, and On the son of Peleth, sons of Reuben, took men; and they rose up before Moses with some of the children of Israel, two hundred and fifty leaders of the congregation, representatives of the congregation, men of renown. They gathered together against Moses and Aaron, and said to them, "You take too much upon yourselves, for all the congregation is holy, every one of them, and the LORD is among them. Why then do you exalt yourselves above the assembly of the LORD?" So when Moses heard it, he fell on his face;
>
> -Numbers 16:1-4

We can't escape who these men are, 250 <u>leaders</u>, representatives, men of renown. Now, let me talk about this word *renown*. This word is used to talk about reputation throughout scripture, it is usually used when talking about the reputation of God Himself. So, this is not that these were just well-known guys. These were notable, respected, competent leaders.

Think of your ten favorite modern church leaders, and imagine they come and challenge the two men you have the most respect for—who you would consider the Moses and

Aaron of our day. These leaders weren't nobodies. Again, several million people are in the desert, and these are some of the top 250 leaders out of millions of available choices. So, they are not a rabble.

Look at Moses' response when they come; he gets down on the ground. He's seen this before and he's seen the results. It's not going to end well, and he knows it. And we need to read what happens here because the rebellion is more open this time, there's more hostility. Now, this is what Moses says to them while he is lying on the ground,

> and he spoke to Korah and all his company, saying, "Tomorrow morning the LORD will show who is His and who is holy, and will cause him to come near to Him. That one whom He chooses He will cause to come near to Him. Do this: Take censers, Korah and all your company; put fire in them and put incense in them before the LORD tomorrow, and it shall be that the man whom the LORD chooses is the holy one. You take too much upon yourselves, you sons of Levi!" Then Moses said to Korah, "Hear now, you sons of Levi: Is it a small thing to you that the God of Israel has separated you from the congregation of Israel, to bring you near to Himself, to do the work of the tabernacle of the LORD, and to stand before the congregation to serve them; and that He has brought you near to Himself, you and all your brethren, the sons of Levi, with you? And are you seeking the priesthood also? Therefore you and all your company are gathered together against the LORD. And what is Aaron that you complain against him?"
>
> -Numbers 16:5-11

So here we can see what is happening. These men are already leaders. They already have positions of authority in the community of God's people, but it's not good enough for them. They feel that they need to assert themselves and take their place, that there is a place of higher authority and responsibility that is rightfully theirs to take. They had Miriam syndrome. Instead of holding their place, something in them makes them want to stake out their territory and take a more forward position.

And Moses reminds them that their current leadership roles are a big deal. They are chosen leaders out of millions to serve the Lord in the tabernacle. And he warns them that who they are aligning themselves against is not Moses and Aaron, it's the Lord. Another thing people fail to see when they are choosing sides in a matter. When we align ourselves against a delegated authority of God, we are not taking a stand against that person, we are taking a stand against their leadership position and authority, and thus against God Himself. All authority comes from God, and if the delegated authorities are telling us to do something, we had better do it, or we are taking a stand against God Himself. People can never seem to make that connection in their minds. They always make it about the person who is in the position, and it's not about that. But if the devil can get us focused on that, we miss the real heart of the matter, and next thing we know we're not only in rebellion, but we're advocating others to be rebellious, too.

> And Moses sent to call Dathan and Abiram the sons of Eliab, but they said, "We will not come up!"
> -Numbers 16:12

So Moses wants them to come out and talk about it, but they are going to dig in their heels; now it's not even open for discussion from their perspective. They are no longer teachable or pliable. They are openly rebellious and stiff-necked. Unfortunately, this is how rebellion goes, even when it happens today. People dig in their heels and then they expect an apology from their leaders and those that have never been rebellious. The deception thickens and twists. They feel justified in their position and the scales on their eyes get thicker. And they have a rebuke for Moses:

> Is it a small thing that you have brought us up out of a land flowing with milk and honey, to kill us in the wilderness, that you should keep acting like a prince over us? Moreover you have not brought us into a land flowing with milk and honey, nor given us inheritance of fields and vineyards. Will you put out the eyes of these men? We will not come up!
>
> -Numbers 16:13-14

Now their hearts are revealed; they despise Moses because he is the true leader and they are not, so they accuse him of acting like a prince. Meanwhile, the Lord has said about Moses that he was one of the humblest men on the planet (Numbers 12:3). And they also blame Moses for missing out on their inheritance. We have been reading how the people made the decisions to be rebellious, and not believe the Lord; no one made them think that way, some people among them told them the opposite, but somehow in these men's minds, it's now all Moses' fault. In their twisted thinking, it was Moses who somehow caused them to lose their inheritance, rather than their own conduct being to blame.

Did you see what happened there? Finger-pointing. Failure to take responsibility for one's own choices. Lack of accountability. Self-justification. It was everyone else's fault. That's deception. And it's a normal outworking of rebellion. Unfortunately, I see it happen the same way, every time. Moses then defends himself with the Lord, and not with the people.

> Then Moses was very angry, and said to the LORD, "Do not respect their offering. I have not taken one donkey from them, nor have I hurt one of them.
>
> -Numbers 16:15

Leaders and potential leaders take note: you don't need to defend yourself; let God do that. And even though Moses was very angry with these leaders, he held his peace and directed his comments to the Lord.

> And Moses said to Korah, "Tomorrow, you and all your company be present before the LORD—you and they, as well as Aaron. Let each take his censer and put incense in it, and each of you bring his censer before the LORD, two hundred and fifty censers; both you and Aaron, each with his censer." So every man took his censer, put fire in it, laid incense on it, and stood at the door of the tabernacle of meeting with Moses and Aaron. And Korah gathered all the congregation against them at the door of the tabernacle of meeting. Then the glory of the LORD appeared to all the congregation.
>
> -Numbers 16:16-19

So this is it, they are going to present themselves before God and let Him decree who He supports. As on previous occasions, the Presence of God and the Glory of God show up. Let's read what happens.

> And the LORD spoke to Moses and Aaron, saying, "Separate yourselves from among this congregation, that I may consume them in a moment." Then they fell on their faces, and said, "O God, the God of the spirits of all flesh, shall one man sin, and You be angry with all the congregation?" So the LORD spoke to Moses, saying, "Speak to the congregation, saying, 'Get away from the tents of Korah, Dathan, and Abiram.'" Then Moses rose and went to Dathan and Abiram, and the elders of Israel followed him. And he spoke to the congregation, saying, "Depart now from the tents of these wicked men! Touch nothing of theirs, lest you be consumed in all their sins." So they got away from around the tents of Korah, Dathan, and Abiram; and Dathan and Abiram came out and stood at the door of their tents, with their wives, their sons, and their little children. And Moses said: "By this you shall know that the LORD has sent me to do all these works, for I have not done them of my own will. If these men die naturally like all men, or if they are visited by the common fate of all men, then the LORD has not sent me. But if the LORD creates a new thing, and the earth opens its mouth and swallows them up with all that belongs to them, and they go down alive into the pit, then you will understand that these men have rejected the LORD." Now it came to pass, as he finished speaking all these words, that the ground split apart under them, and the earth opened its mouth and swallowed them up, with their households and all the men with Korah, with all their goods. So they and all those with them went down alive into the pit; the earth closed over them, and they perished from among the assembly. Then all Israel who were around them fled at

their cry, for they said, "Lest the earth swallow us up also!" And a fire came out from the LORD and consumed the two hundred and fifty men who were offering incense.

-Numbers 16:20-35

The earth splits open, and their families and all they own fall into the pit, and the earth closes over them again. What in the world? Can you imagine the scene? Fire then erupts from the presence of the Lord and He burns these 250 leaders to a crisp. Same rebellion, same result. Devastating consequences. Not a crime, not a murder, not an act of violence on the part of these leaders. Just a posture of the heart and words that demonstrated their rebelliousness to God's authority.

Now I have a phrase I use from time to time when I note certain behavior. It's "stuck on stupid". Well, it could never be more appropriately used than in this instance. Look at what verse 41 says, *"On the next day* (emphasis mine) all the congregation of the children of Israel complained against Moses and Aaron, saying, "You have killed the people of the Lord." Seriously? I mean, let's just think through this logically. So, Moses and Aaron can make fire come out of the Tent of Meeting? Moses and Aaron can make the ground open up, selectively I might add, so that it just consumes the families of the same 250 leaders who got roasted? I mean these people must be stuck on stupid to repeat the same offense as the day before!

But here is the lesson: rebellion is deception and it blinds us. This is how serious it is, that even in the midst of what is happening supernaturally all around them, they CANNOT make the connection. They CANNOT see what's happening here.

After making it a habit of sowing into rebellion, they have been given over to their deception. This is what happens when we believe with all our heart that we are in the right, BUT we are in the wrong.

This is what happens when we are offended, and all kinds of people are telling us we have it wrong, but we insist we have it right. Listen, don't listen to those that agree with you in your offense. If they were any type of friend, they would be telling us to get over our offense. These people have now witnessed four occasions with the same sort of results, and they still don't get it. And what this shows us is the hardening of the heart. Because they have entertained this rebellion, they are now poisoned, once they were poisoned, their hearts hardened. They are tainted, and they cannot see right from wrong, even when it is right in front of their faces, and they behold it with their eyes and hear it with their ears.

And what happens next? The glory of the Lord appears. Oh, boy, here we go again. Are we picking up another pattern here? I thought the glory of the Lord was supposed to be this wonderful experience? I mean, is not another way to say this, the presence of the Lord was manifested? We are people of the presence, are we not? Is that not what people desire to see so much nowadays? The Presence? My brothers and sisters, if we are in rebellion towards the Lord, the presence of God can be a lethal experience for us. Now some will disagree with me and say, "well that was the Old Testament". Maybe so. I wonder if Ananias and Sapphira thought the same thing?

These people were stuck on stupid, and they accuse Moses and Aaron of killing God's people. And again, the Lord says to Moses in verse 45, "Get away from among this congregation, that I may consume them in a moment". God has this thing about consuming people and doing it in a moment. Again, do you see God's perspective towards rebellion? And before Moses and Aaron can even respond, a plague breaks out among the people that brings instant death! Ask yourself, what kind of a plague brings instant death? By the time it takes Aaron to run and get his censor to make atonement for the people, over 14,000 people have died from the plague. Again, atonement is made, but the consequences have been very severe. The bad part about deception is that it's deceiving.

So now we're in Numbers 21, and the Israelites are attacked as they travel by a Canaanite king.

> The king of Arad, the Canaanite, who dwelt in the South, heard that Israel was coming on the road to Atharim. Then he fought against Israel and took *some* of them prisoners. So Israel made a vow to the Lord, and said, "If You will indeed deliver this people into my hand, then I will utterly destroy their cities." And the Lord listened to the voice of Israel and delivered up the Canaanites, and they utterly destroyed them and their cities. So the name of that place was called Hormah. Then they journeyed from Mount Hor by the Way of the Red Sea, to go around the land of Edom; and the soul of the people became very discouraged on the way.
>
> -Numbers 21:1-4

So, I find this story interesting as well. King Arad manages to take some hostages, as we read, but the people of Israel pray to the Lord and then go into battle. They ultimately wipe out all of the Canaanites and have a complete and utter victory over their enemies. But once the battle is over, they fall into discouragement, and they fall right back into their own sinful, complaining, unbelieving ways. You would think that the victory would have prevented them from entering into this posture, but it didn't.

> And the people spoke against God and Moses: "Why have you brought us up out of Egypt to die in the wilderness? For there is no food and no water, and our soul loathes this worthless bread."
>
> -Numbers 21:5

Same situation here as the others, but some key notables to take away from this passage. First, this is the next generation. By the time this event takes place, most of the old generation has died, but the new generation suffers from the same sickness, rebellion, and unbelief. Here's another characteristic of being rebellious. Rebellion is sown into the next generation by your actions. It's bad enough that people are rebellious in their hearts naturally, but it's doubly bad when a child has rebellion sown into them by watching their parents, or their grandparents.

I know a rebellious man. And his children are more rebellious. Instead of accountability throughout the lives of his kids, he continually chose and continues to choose mercy. Instead of consequences, there is always a sweeping under the rug. Listen, I believe in mercy, and I believe in covering a multitude of sins, but there is covering, and then there is covering. God covers. Not to cover up, but to protect. God doesn't excuse, but He also doesn't expose, not if we are repentant.

If we are unrepentant, He still doesn't expose us. He doesn't have to. The sin will eventually expose us. We will expose ourselves. And He will stand by and allow that to happen to us to get us to repentance. And His mercy is inexhaustible, thank the Lord, but it is reserved for those who enter into repentance, not for those who choose rebellion.

Now this man's children are old enough to have their own children, and in all of his grandchildren, there is rebellion. So, there is a third generation of rebelliousness, and as you might expect, it gets worse with each passing generation. The only solution to it at this point is submission, but unfortunately, I don't see that happening. So, rebellion can become a generational curse in your family line if you allow it to take root. That's why it's so important to stay away from this stuff.

And this time, the children of Israel are bolder in a negative way. In the previous instances, the rebellious people spoke against Moses, or Moses and Aaron. This time around, emboldened by their rebellion, they spoke against Moses and the Lord. Secondly, they despised the blessing of the Lord. They called their bread worthless. What was their bread? It was manna. This was the miraculous provision of God for the last 40 years that sustained their physical lives...and they despised it. This is how they survived, and they thought it was worthless. When rebellion is the posture of your heart, even the miraculous provision of God leaves a bad taste in your mouth.

This time, there is no manifestation of glory, but many fiery serpents are sent by the Lord into the camp, and many people are bitten and die. There is a glimmer of hope in this story. The people realize the foolishness of their posture and they repent! Numbers 21:7, "Therefore the people came to Moses, and said, "We have sinned, for we have spoken against the Lord and against you; pray to the Lord that He take away the serpents from us." The Lord then instructs Moses to fashion a serpent out of bronze and raise it on a pole. Whoever looks at it will be healed.

These five occasions have glaringly similar circumstances—complaining, rebellion to authority, and unbelief. In every instance, the Lord responded with two things: death and atonement. As we have seen, many people died each time they entered into rebellion and many people were saved. I am glad the Lord demonstrated His mercy and forgiveness on each occasion, but I also do not gloss over the fact that tens of thousands of people also died.

So, while there was atonement and forgiveness each time, the consequences of rebellion were staggering each time. For the people that were roasted by fire, swallowed by the earth, consumed by a plague, or bitten by a fiery serpent, the atonement had very little impact. It was too late for them. Church, it is a very serious thing to be rebellious. Rebellion has consequences.

This kind of message is easily and casually disregarded. The arguments that modern Christians always appeal to are, 1) This was the Old Testament, 2) Now we have Jesus, and 3) God is love. I agree with all three sentiments, but we are fools if we believe that gives us a pass when it comes to rebellion. God is still God, and the devil is still the devil, and the same, sad story is continuing to play out, just the way it always has.

Yes, it was the Old Testament. But the stories of the Old Testament are there to provide us the examples by which we need to live. In the second letter to Timothy, Paul wrote, "All Scripture is given by inspiration of God, and is profitable for doctrine, for reproof, for correction, for instruction in righteousness" (2 Timothy 3:16). So we cannot read these passages dismissively and say, "that was the Old Testament". These stories are profitable for doctrine. Doctrine is what we believe about the Lord. These stories are profitable for your correction. They are profitable for your instruction.

As I said earlier, God demonstrated His love and forgiveness in each instance, but He also demonstrated that there are serious consequences when we align ourselves with rebellion. I am personally glad that it *seems* God does not respond this way in our day, but I am not so foolish to believe that He has changed His perspective towards rebellion. I think He takes it just as seriously today as He did then.

The point of walking through all of these stories from the Book of Numbers is not because I'm trying to convince you that God will respond to His people in the same way today that He did back then (although I have to admit, the potential still exists). But what I am trying to show you is God's response to the rebellion. And because we are supposed to be being conformed to His image, I believe we should have the same response to rebellion in our own lives. I do not recommend that when we see Christians in rebellion we try and set them on fire. I will also add that what we see in the lives of another believer is generally none of our business. I don't believe the Lord needs more Kingdom police officers. So please, just focus on yourself. I do recommend, however, that whenever we see or are convicted of rebellion in our own lives, that we adopt a similar response to God's response to it. In other words, if we see rebellion in our own life, treat it the way God treated the Israelites in Numbers. Scorch that rebellion with the holy fire of God; kill it, purge it, throw it down into the pit! Have no mercy on it! Don't accommodate it, don't excuse it, don't tolerate it! Go after it with everything you've got until it is purged from among your members. Leave no trace of it! Treat it as though it has offended God and must be removed from your midst immediately! How? Look to Jesus, the same way the Israelites looked upon that snake. We only have any victory over rebellion because of Him.

To the critics' next point, yes, we have Jesus, but Jesus did not die so that we can do what we want. The *default* posture of the Christian should be to submit and obey. But in my years as a pastor, I find that the default posture of some Christians is to rebel and go their own way. Jesus does not condone our rebellion, and we cannot be rebellious and, in our unrepentance, invoke His atonement as our protection from His judgment. The key to obtaining the cleansing by the Blood is repentance.

Yes, God is love. And I am probably more thankful for that than anything else. Thankfully, I have never seen rebellious Christians that I have dealt with instantly burnt to death by fire, swallowed by the earth, consumed with a plague, or bitten by fiery serpents. But what I have seen is people be rejected by the Lord. I have seen spiritual inheritances lost. I have seen missed opportunities for leadership and ministry. I have seen removals of lamp stands. I have seen the Lord's judgment upon many, many people who would not relent—who stiffen their neck versus bending their knee. I have seen rebellion sown into the hearts of children and grandchildren. And I have seen the consequences of trying to live life as a rebellious Christian.

And unfortunately, the rebellion in believers is becoming more prevalent all the time. This is an extremely dangerous thing and unfortunately, saying "I'm sorry" does not always stop the consequences. Be not deceived; God is not mocked: for whatsoever a man soweth, that shall he also reap (Galatians 6:7 KJV).

I stay away from rebellious people. I don't want to be anywhere near it, because it is dangerous, and it is deceiving, and it can infect you. I think of deception as I think of tar or tree sap. Have you ever worked with tar or tree sap? Once it gets on you, it is virtually impossible to get off and invariably, it gets on your clothes and they get ruined, and inevitably you touch some other part of your skin and it gets on there too, and it's just a huge mess. It is so much better not to get anywhere near it.

I tell you another truth, don't ever get near what the Lord hates. The Lord hates rebellion and He hates several other things, too (Proverbs 6:16-19). Don't ever, ever, ever, associate yourself with something the Lord hates. Notice what the Lord said in almost every instance He showed up. "Separate yourselves …, remove yourselves …, get away from these people that I may consume them in a moment." We cannot afford to be involved. Unless the Lord gives us personal instruction and direction to get involved or to try and reach people who are in rebellion, stay away.

Number one, because if He hasn't told us to get involved, we won't be able to reach them. They are in deception, and we will not have the power to break that deception if we are going to them in our power. Number two, we risk becoming infected. We risk their rebellion getting on us.

Some might say, well they need to be saved or someone needs to reach them. I agree, but I don't automatically assume that it's my job to do it. When we believe it's automatically our job to rescue people, we're just being naïve, and more often than not driven by emotion. We forget that God has people everywhere. First, He cares about them as people more than we ever will. So, if He wants to reach them in their deception and rebellion, then He will. He will orchestrate circumstances; He will send people into their lives who are graced to withstand being deceived by their rebellion. He will send people who are not emotionally involved in the situation so they can see clearly and avoid the traps of offense.

In most situations, if we're involved in the issue or have close friends who are involved in the issue, we would be much better served to pray for them, to commit them to God, and to allow Him to rescue them in His way and His timing. But Christians rarely know how to do that. Everyone is always assuming it's their job to save somebody, and they go and get in the Lord's way. Don't do it. Do yourself a favor. Stay out of it, stay away from it, and leave it alone. If the Lord needs us to rescue someone, He will let us know, and He'll let our leadership know. There will be a witness with them that we need to do this. That's the whole point of being under cover—of being under authority so that multiple people can keep us safe and keep us accountable.

There is a man who is nationally known who has recently fallen publicly. While working in my garage on household stuff, the thought came to me very strongly that I am to make contact with him to offer him an opportunity to work through repentance. Now I don't know this guy, I have no relationship with him whatsoever, and the truth is, if I help him, it will probably just mean criticism and accusation for me from other Christians. Which is pathetic, I know, but I'm just sharing that as an example. After I received this impression, the first thing I did was pray about it and run it by my leadership team. So even in a situation that I am not involved with and have no vested interest in, I still submit my impressions to others that I trust to see if what I am receiving bears witness with the Spirit of God in them. I didn't automatically assume I was correct because of the randomness with which this impression occurred to me. God has people everywhere, if He wants to help someone who has lost their way, there are thousands and tens of thousands of people just like me, going about their daily lives, minding their own business, who have their antennae on. Do you know what I mean? I was just casually working in my garage when I got that impression, but my antenna was on. So maybe I can help this guy and maybe I can't, but if the Lord wants me to reach out to him, then who am I to resist the Lord? I'm not emotionally involved in this man's situation, and as I said, if I do get involved there's probably nothing but trouble in it for me from outside critics. But one thing I won't be fooled by because of my perspective is this man's rebellion or his excuses. I won't be emotionally attached to this situation and hopefully, by God's grace, I'll be able to see the field clearly to be of real assistance to him.

This leads to the last thing I want to share about rebellion. It's another story of rebellion, but it's one about taking responsibility upon yourself that is not yours to take. If you read 1 Samuel 15 you can see King Saul decided he wanted to do his own thing. He had a clear instruction from the Lord, but he listened to the people instead. Then he decided that he was tired of waiting on the man of God and took license to do something that he had no authority to do by offering a sacrifice to the Lord. When called out by the prophet Samuel, King Saul tried to make excuses, but it was too late. Saying "I'm sorry" was not going to cut it anymore. I don't want to write out the whole story, but let me set the stage again.

The time has come for the Amalekites to be destroyed. The Lord hated the Amalekites. Amalek was the king who raided Israel as they left Egypt. He would come up on the rear of the group and kill the elderly and the weak who lagged behind the main body of people and would plunder their goods. This angered the Lord significantly. Now all these generations later the Lord is going to wipe out the descendants of Amalek. He has Samuel the prophet tell Saul to go and wipe them out and not spare anything.

> Then Saul said to the Kenites, "Go, depart, get down from among the Amalekites, lest I destroy you with them. For you showed kindness to all the children of Israel when they came up out of Egypt." So the Kenites departed from among the Amalekites.
>
> -1 Samuel 15:6

So here Saul gives a warning to the Kenites to get out early. Remember what I said earlier, don't get around something the Lord hates. So, they leave the area and Saul moves in to destroy the Amalekites, but the people of Israel don't destroy them as the Lord has commanded. They destroy most of the stuff and keep the good things. This is the Lord's response:

> Now the word of the Lord came to Samuel, saying, "I greatly regret that I have set up Saul *as* king, for he has turned back from following Me, and has not performed My commandments." And it grieved Samuel, and he cried out

to the Lord all night. So when Samuel rose early in the morning to meet Saul, it was told Samuel, saying, "Saul went to Carmel, and indeed, he set up a monument for himself; and he has gone on around, passed by, and gone down to Gilgal." Then Samuel went to Saul, and Saul said to him, "Blessed *are* you of the Lord! I have performed the commandment of the Lord." But Samuel said, "What then *is* this bleating of the sheep in my ears, and the lowing of the oxen which I hear?" And Saul said, "They have brought them from the Amalekites; for the people spared the best of the sheep and the oxen, to sacrifice to the Lord your God; and the rest we have utterly destroyed." Then Samuel said to Saul, "Be quiet! And I will tell you what the Lord said to me last night." And he said to him, "Speak on." So Samuel said, "When you *were* little in your own eyes, *were* you not head of the tribes of Israel? And did not the Lord anoint you king over Israel? Now the Lord sent you on a mission, and said, 'Go, and utterly destroy the sinners, the Amalekites, and fight against them until they are consumed.' Why then did you not obey the voice of the Lord? Why did you swoop down on the spoil, and do evil in the sight of the Lord?" And Saul said to Samuel, "But I have obeyed the voice of the Lord, and gone on the mission on which the Lord sent me, and brought back Agag king of Amalek; I have utterly destroyed the Amalekites. But the people took of the plunder, sheep and oxen, the best of the things which should have been utterly destroyed, to sacrifice to the Lord your God in Gilgal." So Samuel said: "Has the Lord *as great* delight in burnt offerings and sacrifices, As in obeying the voice of the Lord? Behold, to obey is better than sacrifice, *And* to heed than the fat of rams. For rebellion *is as* the sin of witchcraft, And stubbornness *is as* iniquity and idolatry. Because you have rejected the word of the Lord, He also has rejected you from *being* king."

-1 Samuel 15:10-23

Now if you're like me, there is still something in you that has questioned the severity of God's wrath to rebellion. Just on the commonsense level, one has to wonder about the justice in it. And here we find the reason why rebellion is so terrible and so serious in the eyes of God. **Rebellion is as the sin of divination.** Other translations read *witchcraft*. *The Message* says it this way:

> Not doing what God tells you is far worse than fooling around in the occult. Getting self-important around God is far worse than making deals with your dead ancestors. Because you said No to God's command, he says No to your kingship.
>
> -1 Samuel 15:23 (MSG)

Let's be plainer. Rebellion is the worship of Satan. Rebellion to authority is sin and worshipping another god. When we rebel, we violate the number one commandment of God. We worship another god. Not only do we worship another god, but we also reject God and accept His number one enemy as god. That is why rebellion is so serious.

Rebellion is not a mild disagreement. It is not one person viewing a matter one way and another person viewing it another way. It is not their preference and your preference. It is the rejection of God and the worship of His enemy, plain and simple. All it took for Satan to get thrown out of heaven like lightning was thinking he would take a place of authority that was not his to take. God's reaction was swift and violent. In like manner, every time His people did not believe in Him, partnered with rebellion, attempted to elect leadership for themselves, or appoint themselves to positions that were not theirs to take, God's response was swift and violent, like lightning. Some scholars believe that when the people of Israel were consumed by fire as recorded in the book of Numbers, that the actual meaning is they were lit on fire by lightning striking them.

Unfortunately, as I continue in ministry, I see all kinds of "believers" that continue to treat rebellion with passivity. They rationalize away their rebellion, justify their actions, and they infect others along the way. They poison leaders with their delusion. And things most often end up in a huge, huge mess. They may not spontaneously combust, but the devastation that follows their lives is very apparent, and their ending will be very similar to those in the wilderness.

What these rebellious "Christians" don't understand is that when their overall posture is rebellion, then everything they do carries the taint of rebellion. When they worship, it stinks of rebellion. When they serve, it's manipulation. When they pray, they usually pray from selfish motives. Those prayers in and of themselves can be rebellious. Do you know who answers rebellious prayers? Not the Lord, but our enemy. The enemy of our souls loves rebellious prayers because without even consciously knowing it, we are committing witchcraft. Next thing we know, the enemy, the demonic, partners with those prayers and furthers his kingdom objectives. Because of rebellion, we've moved from what we thought was a good deed—praying—to committing witchcraft.

You may be thinking that I am implying these rebellious Christians will end up in hell. Well, you should believe that, because that is exactly what I am implying. We cannot live in the house of God and wave the banner of the enemy. When we do not align ourselves in complete submission to the Lord, then we stand in rebellion and allegiance with His enemy. There is no middle ground.

My prayer for us is that we will walk circumspectly. That we will be discerning. That we will be aware of rebellious attitudes in ourselves and others no matter how subtle they may be. My further prayer is that when we encounter rebellion, we will flee from it, that we will not get involved, and we will not try to rescue the people in it. If we feel the Lord is sending us to solve the issue, make sure that we have the witness of trusted leaders around us. We cannot afford to bring judgment on ourselves because we wanted to be helpful. Put your trust in the Lord— only He can do the saving anyway—and let Him work it out. He has people everywhere. Pray for His mercy for those that are rebellious, and ask Him to save them. Pray more importantly that their hearts will be open to receive correction.

In review, rebellion is serious. Rebellion is sneaky. Rebellion is contagious. Rebellion is deceptive. Rebellion is a posture. Rebellion is witchcraft. Rebellion is the worship of Satan. Rebellion has no part in the life of the believer on any level. The greater the role rebellion has in your heart, the lesser your authority will be in the Kingdom of God.

8

DISCIPLINE

For whom the Lord loves He chastens, and scourges every son whom He receives.
-Hebrews 12:6

I believe in two things: Discipline and the Bible. Here you'll receive both.
-Warden Samuel Norton, The Shawshank Redemption

Discipline is not a favorite topic of most Christians. It's not a favorite of worldly people either, but it is what will separate the wheat from the chaff. Discipline is a very necessary topic for us to understand, because like the topic of authority, the church, by and large, has a terrible conception of what discipline is, and what it is not. Somewhere along the way, the church has failed to address this topic appropriately. They stopped speaking about it, they stopped employing it, and they stopped holding people accountable. And like many other topics, whenever there are abuses of it, we take the topic itself and throw it away, versus doing the appropriate thing by keeping the topic and holding the abuser accountable for how they have mishandled what God has given us by His word. It's a tactic of the devil to delegitimize the word of God. We don't get to tear out the pages of the Bible that we don't like and throw them away because someone abused what is said on a given page, or because it runs contrary to our feelings.

Likewise, if people are raised by the hand of an abusive parent, they tend to negate the principles of discipline because of what they experienced. When we do that, we judge the Scriptures by the actions of man, versus judging the actions of man by the Scriptures. That is backward. When we judge the right way, we get to throw out the actions of the person who operated contrary to the Scripture, instead of throwing out the Scripture. We do this by not holding their actions against them and walking in forgiveness when they mess up. And I know that can be tough to do, but that is the appropriate response, and it is possible for us by God's grace (divine enablement).

I hope that everyone reading this realizes discipline is a gift from God. It's a God idea. If not, hopefully by the end of this chapter you'll realize it. Yes, it was given by God, just like authority is given by God. And discipline is dispensed by both God Himself, and by His authorities in the earth (see Romans 13). And we hate when someone abuses authority and discipline, and we want God to immediately step in and rectify the situation, but when we do that, we really just demonstrate how immature we are in our thinking, because the reality is, God does not step in, much to our chagrin. No, He stands by while people misuse what they are given, all the while taking notes, and He stands ready to hold them accountable at the end for how they have used or misused what He has graced them with. And that end may be at THE end, or it may be whenever He ends it for them in that season, but that is God's call to make, and it is not subject to our opinion, review, or approval. And we hate that idea, too, because we want instant justice. Everything has to be fixed right now ... except when it comes to us, of course, and our behavior. We don't want instant justice for ourselves, do we?

No, we want God to be rich in mercy when it comes to us ... longsuffering ... patient, and kind ... He just needs to handle everyone else instantly.

But delegated authorities make mistakes at times and may even abuse their authority. And when they do, our options in response are very limited actually, according to Scripture. I recently heard Bishop Joseph Garlington, Sr. say, while preaching on spiritual authority, "Not submitting is never an option." And I agree emphatically.

God gives us two options. Option #1 is to submit or option #2 is to submit. Those are the only choices. And because we don't trust the authority that God has placed us under (which worked out to its logical conclusion, says we ultimately don't trust God) or when God does not handle everyone instantly in the timing we expect, or by our preferences, then we often take matters into our own hands. And when we take matters into our own hands versus submitting as He requires, we automatically enter into a posture of rebellion regardless of what we think, say, or do next. Whatever action we take will be rebellious, birthed in sin. How far it goes and how much it grows will be completely up to us, but we are in error from the word *Go*!

Some people dethrone God, put themselves in His place, and set about setting things in order the way they think is best. Some do this on an individual scale, and some do it on a corporate scale. Some do it by coming up with man-made ideas and doctrines. They'll deliver popular messages that say God does not discipline us anymore, He just loves us. Or they say that we cannot judge, that's God's job, all we need to do is love. They say cute things like, "why can't we just be left alone?", or "why can't we just leave other people alone and let them live their lives?" They say that God was someone different in the Old Testament than He is in the New Testament. And they come up with excuse after excuse, and reason after reason, to say whatever makes them comfortable, to excuse their behavior, and let them get away with their sin.

And if they don't do that, then they usually leave the place of accountability God has placed them in and go off into rebellion, doing their own thing, claiming that they have heard from God for themselves, or claiming that they have "peace" about their decisions. One of my personal favorites is that they know what God has said in His Word, but He's made an exception in their case or He's given them special permission to do something contrary to His Word. That is heresy. And because they know that sounds silly to even say out loud, they just verse-hunt until they find the verse that fits, take it completely out of context, and apply it to their situation. And because most Christians are biblically illiterate themselves, they fall for all the garbage that gets posted on social media platforms that justifies the rebellion, and they offer sweet encouraging words to the rebel.

I am here to tell the Church that there is a biblical standard of discipline. It's consistent throughout His word, and it is the same as it's always been. And when we neglect to discipline, as parents, and as a church, we set up those we allegedly love and care for, for absolute and total failure.

Let's talk in the parental context first. Why is it important for parents to exercise authority and discipline with their children? Now, I know there will be 20 answers to that question, and most of them are probably correct, but there is an overriding answer. The principal reason that as parents we must discipline our children and exercise our authority over them properly is that

WE are their introduction to God.

Like it or not, the first person we learn or don't learn, discipline from is our parents. The first person we learn or don't learn authority from is our parents. If it is not our parents, it will be whoever cares for us in those young formative years. It could be adoptive parents, grandparents, another relative, guardians, the State, or a system, but whoever is over us when we first begin to learn, is our introduction to authority, and thus God. Now if you ask me, God gets the raw end of that deal from the outset, but it is His program, and He did not ask me for input. Because for most people I know and have counseled, a great part of their problem with God, or how they relate to God, has to do with how they saw or related to their mother or their father, or whoever else I may have mentioned, that is part of their equation growing up. And based on that relationship or the lack thereof, they form ungodly beliefs. And those ungodly beliefs can go awry in many directions. If we had a taskmaster for a father, we could end up with an ungodly belief that God is a taskmaster. Likewise, if we had a spineless father, we could end up with an ungodly belief that relating to God is easy and casual. Both beliefs are ungodly and unbiblical. And ungodly beliefs will mess a person up.

But we are their first introduction to God. And when we fail to discipline, according to the principles of discipline laid out in His book, then those in our care and authority are set up for disaster. Because sooner or later, they will encounter discipline, and sooner or later they are going to encounter authority, and sooner or later they are going to encounter God. And if we love them at all, we don't want their first encounter with God to be their first encounter with discipline. That's why He granted His authority and His discipline to Adam in the garden. We were created to reflect His image and His likeness and to re-present Him in the earth. If we don't discipline those we love, we set them up for failure with the Lord. And to some extent, we will be held accountable for them and the decisions they made because God granted us the ability to create life and be responsible for it. He told Adam:

> ... Be fruitful and multiply; fill the earth and subdue it; have dominion over the fish of the sea, over the birds of the air, and over every living thing that moves on the earth.
> -Genesis 1:28

Subdue it. Have dominion. You see, as a society, as a people, we all crave order. Do you hope that on the way home from work Monday, that you get caught up in a riot? No, of course not. That is not at the top of most of our wish lists. We crave order. Why? Because God is a God of order. Now, no verse in the Bible says that as a quote, but it is demonstrated throughout the Scriptures in everything God does. If you read the book of Exodus and what Moses and Aaron and the priests were to do with the tabernacle, they were to set everything in order before the tabernacle was used.

> The steps of a good man are ordered by the Lord,
> And He delights in his way.
> -Psalm 37:23

What defines the universe? Order. It's the one thing the scientists cannot explain. The universe should be in chaos, but it is not, it is in order. And no matter what theory they try and peddle about the universe's age or how it came into being, the one thing that they absolutely cannot escape or explain away is the order of it. Order is a good thing.

Because God is a God of order and we are made in His image, then we crave order in our being. We crave God. That desire for order was put there by Him, and even the sinful nature cannot overcome the desire for God, and the desire for order, security, and safety. In America, our society is largely a society of order and we are seeing that beginning to change, and I believe the majority of people don't like the change they are seeing. When we drive, we stay on our side of the street. Why? Because if we don't, chaos reigns and someone gets hurt or killed. And when you don't have order in your home, as instituted by discipline and structure, then your children grow up thinking that they are free. Yes and no. Freedom does not equate to lawlessness. You may have heard the expression that freedom is not free, correct? Entirely correct, it is earned. But modern parents have decided that freedom is best, so they give it to their kids without them earning it, and then they wonder why their kids are disasters. They become disasters because they were never taught how to handle the responsibility of freedom. God does not allow us to be free in something until we have learned to bring that thing into subjection.

America is considered a free country, but it is a nation of laws ... some of them are flawed laws no doubt, but the vast majority of them are good and are for our good. Our children, in their freedom, take their lack of respect, their lack of boundaries, their lack of self-control, their mindset that they are free to do whatever pops in their little hearts to do, out into the world of order. And what happens? They run smack dab into the System.

Do you know what the System is? Order. Discipline. The very thing that makes you stop at stop signs and stay on your side of the street. And since it is their first encounter with the requirements of order and discipline, now they find themselves in trouble. And many of them have been ill-equipped to deal with a system of order, discipline, and authority.

If you talk to schoolteachers of today, they will tell you that more than ever, children are out of control. Classrooms are chaos. Disrespect is at an all-time high, large segments of society celebrate disrespect, and teachers have a very difficult time controlling their classrooms. Well of course they do, because the discipline is gone. I believe what the teachers say entirely because I have seen it firsthand in our own children's church classes, so I can just imagine what it is like in public schools. And where do we get off trying to tell the world that Christianity offers a better existence, when church kids look, act, and talk just like world kids?

But our kids will learn discipline, one way or another, and we have choices to make as parents. We can discipline them our way, through our lenses and opinions of what we believe constitutes discipline, or we can teach our kids by God's way, which is laid out in His word. For those children that defy discipline, if the worst-case scenarios play out, there are entire institutions that specialize in discipline. I know because I administrate one. And I have a system of rules, order, and structure there, and that system is non-negotiable. It was prophesied over me once that I stand in the gate of that institution with a high sword. The blade is forged on one side for mercy and the other side for judgment. All those who enter my institution will be afforded mercy first. Those who refuse mercy will find judgment. And do you know what I overwhelming hear from the residents that spend time in my institution? "I feel safe here." Do you know why they feel safe? Because there is order and structure and discipline. And when there is not, the disorder and chaos are responded to in a very quick and efficient manner, and order, structure, and discipline are immediately restored, and then everyone can go back to feeling safe. And I don't restore that order by asking nicely, giving the rebellious ones options, or by telling my staff to excuse their behavior because these nice men are just expressing themselves. Expressing yourself is not an option. Satan expressed himself once and look where it got him. "Well, I just need to be who I am." Yeah, that is called expressing your will. I am not interested in seeing your will, I have already seen it, that's why I am responding. Now you are going to see my will. Korah and company wanted to express themselves to Moses. Moses responded by hitting the deck, and God expressed Himself by engulfing them in flames and by opening up the earth and swallowing their families whole.

When we go to church, we generally feel pretty orderly in the sanctuary. Notice I did not say comfortable. If someone came in and started screaming fire and people got up to run in every direction, everyone's sense of safety would depart, and until order and structure returned our sense of safety would not return, unless we got out of the place where we felt unsafe.

So what does the word of God say about discipline? Well, let's take a look. Because I don't want you to take my word for it. I want you to take His word for it, and I hope that we can dispel the negative connotations of the word *discipline*, and frame it in a life-giving way because discipline is life-giving. See, we automatically—or most people do anyway—when we hear the word *discipline*, for some of us that makes us bristle at the thought. Some, maybe rightfully so, because we have been abused. But the abuse was never, and is never, of God. He does not abuse His people, and He WILL NOT excuse the abuse of His people. The Lord grieves over abuse.

But when we hear the word *discipline*, people often immediately resort to pictures of corporal punishment or abuse, especially if they have had a negative experience with discipline. But discipline does not equal corporal punishment. There is a component of biblical discipline that is corporal punishment for sure, but corporal punishment does not equate to the entire concept of discipline. Not even close. So, the first thing that we have to overcome in our minds, or the first question that we have to answer is, "Is all discipline negative?"

Well, let's ask a different question to see if we can answer this one. Do you believe that you are just the person you should be and that God is finished His work in you? No? I didn't think so. So by saying that, we are all admitting that there is at least a need for discipline. If you will not admit it, I will. I need discipline in my life. Do you want to talk about needs? I need discipline. Why? Because I know me. And a large part of discipline is positive. Proper discipline is positive. I will give some examples.

I have a tree in my yard. It is a young tree compared to the other trees around it. And as a young tree surrounded by older trees, it has to take steps to get the light it so desperately needs to grow. So, what does it do? It bends itself in pursuit of the light. But this bending ultimately is not healthy for it in the long run. So how do I step in to help this young tree? I plant a stake in the ground, tie a rope or a wire to it, tie the other end to the tree, and I *make* the tree stand up tall and straight. Usually, because it can go the other way too far, I also stake it on the other side and tie it in the same manner so now it has to grow up straight. And when I do that, I am *disciplining* the tree to do something it does not want to do. I don't know if the tree is mad at me for that or not, but even if it is mad at me right now, it will thank me later. Because when I have removed its propensity to be bent over, and I have made it to grow straight, it will be stronger and more useful as a straight tree than a bent tree.

But did you notice, the tree is pursuing the light? How could that possibly be bad? It needs light. Why would we restrain it from the light? How does this apply to our lives as Christians? Should we ever be restrained from going after the light? Light is usually associated with the concept of God. Why would we want to be restrained from the light? This would be the scenario when we are pursuing the light, or the ministry, or the opportunity, that we are not ready for. Instead of waiting for the season when we have grown up straight, and our roots have gone down deep, and we are firmly planted. The season when we can sustain the high winds and the tossing to and fro by the storm. **The pursuit of the Light is not justification for growing crooked.**

Two of my children have needed braces on their teeth to correct their teeth alignment, so I allowed an orthodontist to apply discipline to my children's teeth to align them. Their teeth needed straightening. My children have not particularly enjoyed the experience of having braces. I don't know that I have ever met anyone who loved having braces, but I can unequivocally say that those who have reaped straight teeth, even though they hated the experience of braces, really enjoy their beautiful smile.

And you know what? Other people enjoy their beautiful smiles too, but they got there through discipline. Your discipline is not only reaped by you, it is reaped by others.

One of the more common experiences of most parents is teaching their children how to ride a bike. When they first set out to ride a bike, what do parents do to the bike to assist the experience in being a positive one? Right, they put training wheels on the bike. What kind of wheels? Right. Training. You could call them discipline wheels. An odd name I know, but in that case, it is not disciplining the child, it is disciplining the bicycle by not allowing it to go too far one way, or too far the other way. Why? Because if it does, the child would be engaged in an undisciplined activity and they would get hurt. Notice that you don't only put a training wheel on one side of the bike. And what is interesting to me about training wheels is how long they stay on the bike. Some children take right to it and those wheels come off within weeks. But I have even seen children who learn to ride, but they will not let the training wheels come off because, without them, they would be afraid they will fall. Now can anyone say that staking a tree to make it grow straight, applying braces, or putting on training wheels is inappropriate or unnecessary, harsh or hurtful? Of course not. The conclusion we can make then is that not all discipline is bad.

Here are some of my personal favorites when it comes to discipline. "Son, close your mouth when you eat." "Hey son, you need to cover your mouth when you cough." "Don't talk with your mouth full." "Stop yelling." "Please sneeze into a tissue or cover your mouth and nose." "Don't talk when someone else is talking; that's rude." "Wash your hands when you are done going to the bathroom." "Watch your mouth." "Quit running in church." "Say 'excuse me' when you burp." "Don't talk to me with that tone of voice." "Get off the furniture." "Keep your voice down."

All of that is discipline. It is a positive, shaping, formative discipline. What it is, is instilling the principle of self-control, a fruit of the Spirit. **There is no fruit of the Spirit called *freedom*.** There is no fruit of the Spirit called, "I don't want them to feel bad" and there is no fruit of the Spirit that says, "I am your dad, let's be friends." Sorry. I know that does not mesh with our Americanized gospel. All of those things I mentioned are self-control issues, so discipline is not just a negative situation. **Discipline helps conform us into the image of Christ.** To wit, to not discipline does not conform us to the image of Christ.

Now let's see what God's word says about discipline.

Therefore we also, since we are surrounded by so great a cloud of witnesses, let us lay aside every weight, and the sin which so easily ensnares us, and let us run with endurance the race that is set before us, looking unto Jesus, the author and finisher of our faith, who for the joy that was set before Him endured the cross, despising the shame, and has sat down at the right hand of the throne of God. For consider Him who endured such hostility from sinners against Himself, lest you become weary and discouraged in your souls. You have not yet resisted to bloodshed, striving against sin. And you have forgotten the exhortation which speaks to you as to sons: "My son, don't despise the chastening of the Lord, Nor be discouraged when you are rebuked by Him; For whom the Lord loves He chastens, And scourges every son whom He receives."

-Hebrews 12:1-6

Verse 5 reveals for us why we have such problems with topics such as this: three words ... You have forgotten. We forget in our hearts, the basics of life, especially when times get hard. We have an unrealistic expectation that since we are saved, and we belong to the household of faith, life is not supposed to be hard, challenging, and difficult at times. The people of Israel had it, too. They did not expect God to allow difficult times to arise. And if we are honest with ourselves, the majority of the time that we find ourselves dejected, rejected, or disappointed, it is because of our unmet expectations. You have forgotten. The reality is, bad things do happen, and the Lord does allow them. Yes, He has the power to stop them, but sometimes He does not. And because He is just, sometimes He *cannot*. Because if He did, He would stop your bad things too. And like the justice statement I made a few chapters ago, we are all about the idea of Him stopping someone else, we just don't want that same restraint or justice applied to us. See the idea that God should stop all bad things is gormless. That means *lacking intelligence*. If He steps on the scene to put a stop to things, the game is over—their game and yours. And one day that is going to happen, but it is only going to happen once, and it is going to be very, very, very final when it does. So instead of that happening, the devil perpetuates this idea that life is not fair, and we are getting hosed. He does this to try to bring you into offense and instill in you a hatred of God and His authorities. People say, "I cannot serve a loving God who would let this happen or that happen." I understand that the devil has deceived people who say things like that. They would rather see things played out in their version of justice versus trusting in His ultimate justice. In effect, they have just said that they know better than God does. They might want to get that pride in check before they hurt themselves.

The facts of the matter are, we are to blame for the suffering that is on the earth, not the Lord. It was our sin that brought it here and it is our sin that has let it continue to promulgate through the earth. Don't say you cannot serve a loving God who would let this happen. Say you cannot serve a world that continues to promote evil.

> And you have forgotten the exhortation which speaks to you as to sons: "My son, don't despise the chastening of the Lord, Nor be discouraged when you are rebuked by Him; For whom the Lord loves He chastens, And scourges every son whom He receives."
>
> -Hebrews 12:5-6

These verses are quoting Proverbs 3:11–12, "My son, don't despise the chastening of the Lord, Nor detest His correction; For whom the Lord loves He corrects, just as a father the son in whom he delights". Chastening is not the only reason God allows difficult times, but it is an important one. Sometimes, God allows us to go through difficult times, just so that we can be a comfort to someone else down the road, so we know what it's like to be in their shoes, and so we know how to show compassion. Now let's examine the key words of these verses to give us a context of what they mean, instead of just using our imagination to postulate what we think it means. Chastening. The Greek word for chastening is *paideia*. This is what the word means and how it is used in the Bible: the whole training and education of children (which relates to the cultivation of mind and morals, and employs for this purpose now, commands and admonitions, reproof and punishment). It includes the training and care of the body. It also means: whatever in adults cultivates the soul, especially by correcting mistakes and curbing passions. Instruction that aims at increasing virtue. Tutorage, i.e. education or training; by implication, disciplinary correction: —chastening, chastisement, instruction, nurture. This same Greek word is used four times in this chapter of Hebrews, we have seen it in verse 5, and we will see it again in verses 7, 8, and 11. Thus, it would be acceptable for verse 5 to read, "My son, don't despise the discipline of the Lord."

Another verse in which we see this Greek word is Ephesians 6:4, "And you, fathers, don't provoke your children to wrath, but bring them up in the training and admonition of the Lord." So we see it translated as *training* in this verse. It is also commonly seen as the word *nurture,* and it can also be "discipline and admonition of the Lord". The next occasion in which we see it used is 2 Timothy 3:16, "All Scripture is given by inspiration of God, and is profitable for doctrine, for reproof, for correction, for instruction in righteousness." *Paideia* is the word "instruction" in this verse in 2 Timothy. So by biblical definition, discipline encompasses training, instruction, discipline, teaching, cultivating, nurture, chastisement, correction, and restraining. Notice there is nothing about freedom, expression, doing what you want, not feeling repressed, etc.

The verse goes on, "nor be discouraged when you are rebuked by Him." Let us look at the word *rebuke* as well, because this is another word that bristles people's feathers automatically and causes them to think the worst. The Greek word for rebuke is *elegchō,* and it means "to convict, refute, confute, generally with a suggestion of shame of the person convicted, by conviction to bring to the light, to expose." It also means, "to find fault with, to correct." Under *correct*, there are two ways this correction happens. The first type of correction is *by word*, meaning, to reprehend severely, chide, admonish, reprove and to call to account, show one his fault, or demand an explanation. Not very flowery. The other way to correct is *by deed*, meaning to chasten, to punish. So, a rebuke can be verbal or physical. *Elegchō* is used 18 times in 17 verses in the New Testament. In 66% of its uses, or 12 verses out of 17, the context is Christian leaders rebuking Christians. In 28% of its uses, or 5 verses out of 17, the context is Christians rebuking the world or sinners, and in 6% of its uses, or one verse, the context is Jesus asking the Pharisees why they are rebuking Him. So, in 94% of the New Testament verses on rebuke, the context is Christians who are ordered to rebuke fellow believers, the world, or sinners for errant ways and behavior. So much for the whole "not judging" argument espoused by large segments of the American Church.

In other words, part of our responsibility before the Lord, according to His Word, is to bring correction or to bring discipline. Now, bringing correction does not equate with being rude, nasty, condescending, or insulting. That is unacceptable. Likewise, it does not equate with being accommodating, tolerant, lenient, open-minded, or telling others what they want to hear.

And notice what our responsibility is in this, when we are the ones on the receiving end: "nor be discouraged when…". In other words, when we are convicted, refuted, confuted, chided, admonished, reproved, called to account, or shown our faults, our role should not be self-defense, deflection, and avoidance. Remember, we have not resisted to the point of bloodshed. That is God's threshold for hearing us whine. Consider Jesus; we are not bleeding. Your responsibility is to not be discouraged. Now how is that possible? One way and one way only … by choice. We choose our reaction to the correction. God says it is a good thing to be corrected, and He says we are not to be discouraged by said correction. Why should we not be discouraged? Hebrews 12:6, "For whom the Lord loves He chastens, And scourges every son whom He receives." The Lord also says this Himself in Revelation 3:19, "As many as I love, I rebuke and chasten. Therefore, be zealous and repent." So, the why of why we should not be discouraged is that because His chastisement of us demonstrates His love for us and lets us know that we are a son. Verse 8 of Hebrews 12 says, "But if you are without chastening, of which **all** (emphasis mine) have become partakers, then you are illegitimate and not sons." Let me be frank, if we are without chastening, then we are bastards and not sons. There is no way around it. There is no flowery spin to put on it. It is not politically correct, and it will not sell many books, but it is Gospel. And everybody gets their turn at the wheel. All have become partakers. The only choice we have is how we respond.

Now in verse 6, the word for *chasten* is the same Greek root word as in verse 5, but there are some differences. In verse 6, it is *paideuō* instead of *paideia*. The first definition is "to train children, to be instructed or taught or learn, to cause one to learn." The second definition is "to chastise, to chastise or castigate with words, to correct; specifically of those who are molding the character of others by reproof and admonition." The next definition is used exclusively when speaking of chastening by God and it means: "to chasten by the affliction of evils and calamities." There are some current leading movements in Christianity in America that would take issue with that definition. Sorry, I am just a fact reporter. The third meaning is, to chastise with blows, to scourge, of a father punishing his son, of a judge ordering one to be scourged.

The last part of this verse reads, "...and scourges every son whom He receives." How many sons? Every. In Greek, the word for *scourge* means "to scourge." There is a one-word alternative. It is the shortest definition of a Greek word I have personally ever seen in a biblical word study. The other word is *flog*. So, this verse can be translated, "For whom the Lord loves, He chastises with blows, like a judge ordering one to be scourged, and he flogs every son whom He receives." That would be a genuine interpretation, in the New Testament, for an aspect of the discipline of God.

I can hear you already, "But pastor, I just don't believe God would do that. I mean He took out all His anger on the cross on Jesus, so He doesn't have to do that anymore." Well, I am pretty sure that Hebrews was written under the inspiration of the Holy Spirit a few decades after the whole Cross situation. And here is the flaw in the statement, "He took out all His anger." God does not discipline out of anger. And because of our human authorities, who usually do, we project that onto God. God's discipline is done out of love always. And because He loves us, He does discipline us. Hebrews 12:9, "Furthermore, we have had human fathers who corrected us, and we paid them respect. Shall we not much more readily be in subjection to the Father of spirits and live?"

Shall we not much more readily be in subjection? When we despise the Lord's chastening, we are putting ourselves on equal ground with God, versus putting ourselves in the position of a son. In effect, we challenge His authority when we despise His chastening. Resentment at chastening reveals to us how we see

God, and how we see ourselves.

Hebrews 12:10, "For they indeed for a few days chastened us as seemed best to them, but He for our profit, that we may be partakers of His holiness." Human fathers cannot discipline perfectly, and there is no expectation on God's part that they can. Notice, the Lord does not dispel the concept of discipline because it will be done in error. Even with the best intentions, I have made mistakes in disciplining my children, but to neglect discipline altogether for fear of mistakes would be far worse a sin committed against them. God can chasten us perfectly because He has perfect knowledge and perfect methods, but if we don't prepare those we love with the mindset that it is okay to be disciplined, then they will not understand how to receive correction from a loving Father who makes no mistakes. If you are a parent, I hope that you realize the gravity of the responsibility you have been given.

Hebrews 12:11, "Now no chastening seems to be joyful for the present, but painful; nevertheless, afterward it yields the peaceable fruit of righteousness to those who have been trained by it." Now, these verses have been about the chastisement we receive from the Lord. There have been times that I have been chastised directly by the Lord. There have been also times I have been properly chastised by superiors, bosses, and elders in the faith; that can also be the chastisement of the Lord. There are times I have also been properly chastised by brothers in the faith, and even those under my authority. That can also be the chastisement of the Lord. The chastisements that have been the most painful have been from the ones under my authority. Not because they were wrong, but because they were right, and because I was guilty of not doing right by them. That is not joyful, that is painful, but when we allow it to have its place, it yields the fruit of righteousness and we have less of a chance of making that mistake again. Discipline is not supposed to be joyful. It is supposed to hurt, and it is supposed to get our attention. If our discipline style does not involve any sting, then we are not disciplining scripturally. And I don't necessarily mean physical punishment, because sanctions, for lack of a better word, can hurt. But I also don't mean an absence of physical punishment either. What good would it do, to discipline my children, if they came away from the experience saying, "Wow! That was joyful and a great time. Let's do that again real soon."? It is the same with the Lord. There was nothing in those definitions of those Greek words that conveyed anything less than an unpleasant experience. The point of unpleasantness is not suffering for the sake of suffering. The point is suffering so that we don't have any desire to go back there again. We have nerves in our body that respond to unpleasant stimuli to train us not to repeat whatever it is that we are doing. I've never met anyone who burnt their hand, threw out their back, or stubbed their toe talk about how it was a joyful experience.

Discipline is important. There are Christians I know that seemingly live their lives from one crisis to the next. When those crises are self-inflicted, I can usually say with some certainty that it is because they are blind to the chastening of the Lord, or they are resisting it. They don't allow the circumstance to train them, change their perspective, or produce repentance. When that happens, the peaceable fruit of righteousness does not grow. And discipline is not always a quick process, and neither is growing the fruit of righteousness. I cannot plant an immature fruit tree and then expect to see fruit on it in two months.

There is much more I could write concerning discipline, but what I hope you can take away from this chapter is the principle that discipline is of the Lord, and discipline when properly employed can produce in us fruit that nothing else can. I also hope that you take away what a sobering responsibility it is before the Lord to discipline your children. It is not a childhood issue. It is not an issue about other people's opinions on the topic. **Discipline is an issue of eternal significance and eternal consequence.**

And there may be some people reading this, who have already missed the opportunity to rightly discipline their children. Or maybe they have an uphill fight to restore order. Maybe they are feeling guilty. Maybe they are reaping, or have reaped, the consequences of ungodly belief about authority and discipline, or maybe they just did not know any better. What now? What now is you repent, you ask and receive forgiveness, you walk in the freedom of forgiveness, and you use your testimony to the best of your ability to warn others. We leave the redeeming of the time, and your kids, to the Lord. He can restore the years that the locusts have eaten, for He is rich in mercy and abounding in grace. So set your heart right with God if it is bent out of shape in any way. We cannot afford to look at discipline in an unhealthy manner, or the chastisement of the Lord with ungodly beliefs.

I don't write about this topic because I was raised by a taskmaster, or because I was in the military, or because I have had a career in Corrections, or because I am a warden, or because I have done everything right. I write about this topic from a posture of not wanting to see what can happen to you or your kids when we neglect the Word of God. Unfortunately, I get to see the effects of that every day. And I have had people laugh at me openly because of my views on discipline, and I have had people ignore what I have to say. They are not laughing as much when they are asking me for counsel years later because their children are out of control or headed to jail. It is not about me anyway; it is about Him and what He has to say.

9

MY LESSON IN AUTHORITY

A man's heart plans his way, But the Lord directs his steps.
-Proverbs 16:9

I wish I could convey to every person I know how important it is to be obedient and submitted to authority. I believe in what I am writing 150%. My life is a living testament to these principles. I believe in them so much; they guide my every decision. My life has been immensely successful on every front, and I experience crazy favor from the Lord everywhere I go, but all of the credit goes to God. He has disciplined me, and I have yielded, and my life is the result. I was not always submitted. I was not always obedient. I was not an obvious rebel on most occasions. I was a closet rebel. I knew better than to pick certain fights and vocalize my rebellion in certain ways, but rebellion lived inside of me, as it lives inside of you.

When I was 18, the Lord put it into my heart to join the military. Oh, at the time I thought it was my wonderful idea to escape the environment I knew, and launch myself out into the big, wide world. Even though rebellious, I wanted with everything in me to be a police officer, but you had to wait until you were 21 years old to apply, and I was only 18. What to do in the meantime? So, I reasoned that a stint in the military police would prepare me for that role and make me a better applicant for police work than most. So, I signed up for the Army in 1994 and left for basic training in February of 1995. Two weeks into basic training, I found out that I was not qualified to be a military policeman. You see, I was a Canadian citizen at the time, in the American Army, and the Army did not entrust positions like being a military policeman to foreign nationals. My choices were to change to a different job specialty in the Army or to go back home.

A few weeks earlier, when I had just arrived in basic training, I learned others in my company were going into Corrections. I did not know what that was at the time and soon found out that was for people who worked in jails and prisons. So, when I found out that I could not be a military policeman, I asked if I could be moved into Corrections instead. I reasoned that the field was related to police work and it still might give me a great chance of being a good police department applicant.

I vividly remember my company commander flipping through the Army regulation on his desk that outlines the qualifications for each job specialty in the Army. He found the Corrections section and reviewed it. He pointed on the page to the first qualification. "All applicants must first meet all of the requirements of a military policeman to be in Corrections," he said. My heart sank. Then my commander said, "Maybe we can get this citizenship requirement waived. Would you like me to put in a request for a waiver to the requirements for you so you can go into Corrections?" I could not say *yes* fast enough. My commander was direct with me. He told me it may not work and may not get approved, but he said in the meantime that I was to train with the other soldiers entering Corrections, and we would keep our fingers crossed. Twelve weeks later I received word that my waiver had been approved.

Now, did you catch what happened? Because I did not, not for about six years. If my commander could put in a waiver for the citizenship requirements to be in Corrections, why could he not put in a waiver for the same requirement to be a military policeman? As I said, that thought did not occur to me for another six years. I would find out later that the waiver I received in basic training was not authorized by Army regulation because citizenship requirements could not be waived. I was technically in the Army fraudulently (on the part of the government) because I had been granted that waiver. I was told that I would have to change my occupation in the Army or be put out of the service, but by then not many people cared. I did not want out of the Army and I did not want to leave Corrections. My battalion commander at the time supported me entirely and refused to make an issue out of it, so she saw to it that the issue was dropped, and I continued in the Army for almost another three years. Looking back, what I know now, is that it was the hand of the Lord on my life. He knew I needed discipline, and for what He was calling me to do, He knew I needed a double dose. See, Corrections is a paramilitary environment. Prisons are jungles and they can only function properly and safely when they are disciplined and orderly. Its citizens comprise the most unruly and rebellious our society has to offer. So not only did I get the discipline of the Army, but I got the discipline of the much more structured and orderly environment of prison on top of that.

And I am so thankful to God even still today because of what He did for me in my military career. He disciplined me and he broke my will using the U.S. Army, the field of Corrections, and some very good and very bad leaders along the way. And in each assignment, I was stretched and disciplined more and more. I learned from good leaders what to do and not do, and I learned from bad leaders what to do and not do. And I excelled. When I was rebellious, my troubles were compounded and the discipline was more severe, and when I learned my lessons and took my lumps, the discipline would relent. And I went through some of those lessons over and over again until I got it. And I still am learning lessons. I am now an apostolic leader and a senior warden and I still have to choose submission from time to time when my flesh would rather be in rebellion. But to learn how to be a good number one, I had to learn to be a great number two.

My first military assignment in the Army, and Corrections, was in Alaska, at a small jail that served as a pre-trial facility for military offenders awaiting court-martial. In this assignment, I met a leader who would change my life. He was a firebrand of a soldier; smart, competent, and capable. He stood head-and-shoulders above everyone else. He was promoted through the ranks at a neck-breaking pace, far outpacing his peers. He was a natural-born leader, and I don't know anyone who did not want to be under his command.

Over the next eleven years I would be assigned around him, but never to him. So, I worked with him in various capacities all that time, but never directly for him. Finally, in 2006 I got my chance. I had left military service in 2003 and he had retired from the Army in 2006. I was in the Midwest and he had taken a job on the East Coast. His place of employment was challenging, and he had been brought in to clean it up. He learned soon thereafter that he would need help, someone he could rely on and trust. Knowing my reputation for integrity and discipline, he called me one day out of the blue and offered me a job. It would mean relocating my family in our first three years of marriage, and with two children, two and under. The long story short is I accepted, and together, he and I revitalized the department where we worked and set it on the right path. To this day, people I run into still reminisce how that department was never so well-run as when he and I were running it.

Over the next four years, I would continue to follow this leader in varying capacities, taking on challenge after challenge. He would be sought out to be the #1 leader of a company or a division, and he would bring me in right behind to be the #2. And a solid number two I was. I blindly followed his every move. I did whatever he told me, and I never questioned his authority. There were times he would make me nervous because his behavior would be erratic, but I would quickly push that out of my mind because after all, he was my #1 leader, I had followed his lead for 15 years, and he was so successful. By following his lead, I was becoming successful, too. After just a few short years, we both had a national reputation in the field of Corrections.

In 2011, things began to spiral downward. He became increasingly hostile to those around him, me included. He began to become paranoid that people were attempting to oust him. He would have fits of rage where he would make grandstanding speeches reminding everyone that he was in charge. He would bark orders and terminate anyone who did not follow his guidance and direction. I was more concerned about his health than anything else because of the erratic nature of his behavior at times, but I often dismissed it as pressure from the job. As far as reminding people that he was in charge, and terminating those who did not follow his orders, that was okay by me. I believed (by this time) in the rule of authority, and I had unquestioned loyalty to him, and because I always did what I was told to do, I had no fear of his authority in my life.

In early 2012 things got bad. Now this man's hostility was turned on me as much, or more often, than anyone else. There was no explanation for it, and I often lay awake at night wondering what was going on with him. One night I was walking across my basement complaining to the Lord about him, and the Lord stopped me cold. He said to me as clear as I have ever heard anything, "Why don't you try praying for him, versus complaining about him?" I never complained about him again. I began to pray for him continually, interceding that the Lord would vindicate him with those who challenged his authority and questioned his decisions. I prayed for the peace of God in his life and blessing on his family. Anything I could think of to pray for him that was a blessing or request for favor, I prayed. The more I prayed, the worse things got. His hostility bloomed. He would give me more responsibility or more authority one minute, and the next minute strip it away. He would yell at me for seemingly minor things, but the next day tell me I was the only one he could trust. It was a really strange time. I felt like a yo-yo.

What was worse was his relationship with those above him in the chain of command. Those relationships were eroding every day, and he was convincing all of us that those above him were stupid and that they were not worth listening to because they did not have the experience that he had. He became a rebel, and he began to openly express rebellion, and he was openly hostile towards his leaders. It got so bad that one day I came home and told my wife that she should be prepared for my termination. Shocked, she asked me why. And I told her that the bosses were getting tired of this man and they were going to get rid of him. I could feel it coming. And I told her, when he goes, they will get rid of me, too.

See, another thing this man did was control all forms of communication. He would not allow his subordinates to communicate with his leaders and vice versa. So I told my wife that all those men knew about me was that this man had hired me and brought me on, so I reasoned that when they would get rid of him, they would get rid of me, too. I remember telling her that there was no way they would ever think I would be loyal to the company if he got removed.

One day he came to me with an olive branch. He apologized for his behavior and temper and reaffirmed his commitment to me. I expressed to him that I was concerned for him and his health. His father had died in his forties of a brain tumor, and I was genuinely concerned that he was maybe having a similar problem. It was the only thing I could think of to explain his erratic behavior. I begged him to go to the doctor and at least get a checkup. He laughed it off and told me he was fine, but he did tell me that he was tired of his bosses, and he was looking to go on to our next challenge, and once again, he wanted to take me with him. I pledged my loyalty to him yet again and said, "Where you go, I go. You just say the word." So, he told me that he had an opportunity to go to another organization, but there was a hurdle if I was to go with him. In working for our current organization, he had signed a contract, and one of the stipulations of that contract was that if he quit, he could not have communication with any of his former employees. It was a safeguard to prevent him from taking valuable staff with him. So he said that for me to go with him this time, he would need me to quit my job before he could quit his, otherwise he could be sued for contacting me if he left employment first. Eager to please, I told him that would be fine, but I would have to be sure about our next steps because my wife was pregnant, and I needed my job. He told me that he would let me know when the time was right. And I pledged to do my part and follow.

As things like this usually go, one day they (the bosses) had enough, and they made the man that I had unquestionably followed for years go away, and just like that, it was over. The way I found out was I was sitting in church on a Sunday morning. My cellphone was ringing from a phone number I did not know, so naturally, I did not answer it. After the third or fourth repeated call from the same number, I figured it must be important, so I left the church service and took the call. I was informed that my boss was no longer with the company, and I was offered his position as the warden effective immediately. I was stunned, and after a brief conversation with my wife, I accepted the position, all the while feeling a sense of disloyalty to the man who had been my biggest mentor. But my wife and I had a baby on the way, our fourth, and as my wife pointed out so gracefully when I told her about the phone call, they could have been calling to fire me, but they were not.

Over the next six months, I learned what was going on right under my nose. A few weeks after becoming the warden, I found a camcorder in my new office with about 30 days' worth of video on it. The recording from each day was my former boss's office in the pitch dark. The video would start with him turning on the camera, placing it under his desk, and leaving the office with it recording. I was confused by this because there were days and days of this dark footage of his empty office but given the strange behavior before his departure, it was just one more thing in a long list.

So I went down to the human resources manager's office to tell him about it and I asked him if he knew what it was. To my surprise, he told me he did know. Intrigued, I pressed for an answer. The Human Resource manager told me that the man I had been blindly following for fifteen years had been trying to fire me for the last six months. I could not speak. Somewhere along the way, this man had descended into utter delusion and paranoia. He had suspected, among other things, that I was breaking into his office and rifling through his things at night. He had set up hidden cameras to catch me. He had expressed frustration to the HR manager that he had not been able to catch me on camera. Well, he could not catch me because it wasn't happening, but that first bit of revelation threw the door wide open, and the scales fell off my eyes. I would begin to see over the next six months all the schemes, and all the ways my mentor tried to "kill" me. One day, overwhelmed by the latest revelation, I said out loud to the Lord, "I was serving King Saul".

And it was true. It did not surprise me ultimately (my middle name is David) that I was neck-deep in my own Saul and David experience. One day I severely lost my temper at the Lord. I remember yelling and pointing at the sky, "You knew, and You kept me blind!" "You knew, and You kept me blind," I repeated at the top of my lungs. I was so angry. It did not take me too much longer to realize that was the Lord's grace toward me. He kept me blind to everything happening under my nose; the mistreatment, the gossip, the slander, the plotting of my demise in the job sense, everything. I was blind as a bat; blindly loyal. Everyone around me knew it and could see it except for me.

I served my boss with blind loyalty. I defended his actions where and when I could with others, attributing his missteps to pressures of the job, leadership, and stress. Turns out, people all around me knew he was plotting my death, but I was so loyal to him, people would not tip me off. I would eventually learn that he told our bosses of his intentions to fire me, and it was three men I did not know and had not very often spoken to, that stayed his hand and would not allow my termination. The same three men, he tried to convince me were our enemies and ones we had to watch out for. Turns out because they stopped him from firing me, he had come up with the idea to have me quit the job first, so he could follow after. It was a trap, and he had no intention of quitting. If I had followed through, I would have quit, and he would have stayed. It was sick, twisted, perverted manipulation. If the Lord had not blinded me to all that was going on, no doubt I would have known and quit, and it would have moved me away from the purpose God had for me. It was a valley I had to travel through. A lesson I had to learn. And I will forever be grateful to the Lord for it.

Hear me on this, Church, what the Lord did for me through all of that, was keep me from sinning against authority. Because I was so blind, even in the face of mistreatment, I was loyal and I was obedient to this man's every command, and so I remained pure. My motives were pure, my actions were pure, and because I walked in integrity, the Lord preserved me entirely, and I did not even know what was happening. So, I take no credit for my actions. It was the discipline of the Lord, through the military, and what He took me through for years, that prepared me not to fail at this moment.

Over the next six months or so, I had to work through forgiveness. I knew if I did not, bitterness would consume me. So, every time I was tempted to get angry and bitter, I would pray for blessings on this man and his family. I would cry for him and pray that the Lord would save him from himself.

One thing I did not mention earlier is that the whole time I knew and served this man for fifteen years, he professed to be a Christian.

10
SUBMISSION TO AUTHORITY

Let every soul be subject to the governing authorities. For there is no authority except from God, and the authorities that exist are appointed by God.
-Romans 13:1

Submission is never optional.
-Bishop Joseph L. Garlington, Sr.

Now we turn our attention to probably the toughest chapter to swallow, and the most comprehensive in the book. In this chapter, I am going to examine submission to authority. When we run afoul of the principles of submission and authority, rebellion is the result. Rebellion is the worship of the devil, and as believers, we should want no part in it. As you can see from the previous chapter, I have lived my authority lessons. What I recounted for you does not scratch the surface of the mistreatment, betrayal, abuse, and manipulation I suffered at the hands of my mentor. But you know what? My abuse does not matter.

What I did not do, in the aftermath of that situation, was give myself the liberty to live in rebellion the rest of my life. I could have taken my experience, internalized it, and made it into a weapon and shield with which to defend myself, and keep at bay, all future leaders. I could rationalize rebellion for the rest of my life as something I need to do to protect myself and my family. I have every reason in the world to never trust a leader again, even Christian leaders. But you know what? I did not do that. And I don't say that with pride; I say it by God's grace. I thank the Lord for my experience. It was one of the best experiences of my life if I am honest, because of what it taught me in hindsight.

The other thing I did not do, was throw away the principles of submission to authority because of how I was treated by a man. The principles of authority come from God. They don't cease to be principles because people use, or misuse them to lord over, or mistreat other people. That man treated me horribly, but that treatment did not negate my obligation to obey and be submitted. He never asked me to do anything illegal, unethical, or immoral, which is where the Bible draws the line on obedience and submission to authority.

I was talking with someone recently who is disillusioned by parachurch ministry. They related that due to being employed in a parachurch ministry with a bad leader, they were ready not only to swear off all parachurch ministry, but organized church, and leaders, too. They want to go it alone. I'm sorry, but we cannot take that position and call ourselves a believer and a follower of Jesus. The Bible outlines for us the expectations of Christians in just about every facet of life. First Peter 2:18 says to be submitted to your masters, not only the good ones, but the harsh ones. It even says we are expected to be beaten if we mess up, and there is no reward for that. The only time we are rewarded for mistreatment is when we are mistreated and our conduct was actually good. Nowhere does the Scripture say that we get to throw off our responsibility to be obedient to the

Word of God because we were treated badly. The unfortunate thing is, most Christians believe that because their leaders or their churches do a bad job of leading, or don't meet their expectations, they are somehow freed from their responsibility to do what the Bible says. I'm sorry, it does not work that way.

Some of you may already be coming out of your skin by what I just said. Some of you may think it could never be God's will that you be mistreated. But let me ask you a question. For three years our Lord lived, ate, walked, taught, worked, and laughed with the one who would betray him. He also bore the sins and betrayal for everyone for all time, and He never did a thing wrong in His life. Do we deserve better treatment? Because if we think we do, we should be repenting for our stinking pride right now before we read another word.

And I think I have heard the whole array of excuses for rebellion. All of these reasons are excuses wrapped in lies from hell. Christians are so foolish when it comes to the lies with which they partner to justify their rebellion. I said earlier in the book that a Christian's default position should be to submit and obey. That seems easy and simple enough, but I find that Christians do all kinds of other action steps first. One of the first things they do is evaluate whether or not the authority telling them to do something is worthy of obedience. Usually, this is a question of respect. Do I value this person or this entity? Do I respect this person? Is this authority figure worthy of my submission and obedience? Well, I can help you avoid all of that needless exercise. The Bible says:

> Every person is to be in subjection to the governing authorities. For there is no authority except from God, and those which exist are established by God. Therefore

whoever resists authority has opposed the ordinance of God; and they who have opposed will receive condemnation upon themselves.

-Romans 13:1-2

There is no translation needed for this verse, but let me point out some of the highlights. This command is not just for Christians. This verse applies to "every person". And every authority that exists, good, bad, or indifferent is from God. There is no qualifier on their position as an authority based on their behavior. In other words, if we think a leader is wrong or even evil, it does not exempt us from submitting to them and obeying them because they are from God, whether we like it or not. **Injustice is not an excuse for rebellion.** And the wicked nature in us cannot stand to hear that. It infuriates people to no end.

American culture has taught us that we have a right to not be abused and mistreated. That we have a right to throw off our oppressors. That we have a right to call our shots and do our own thing. Only if we agree do we submit! Well, I can tell you, there is no more satanic ideal in existence. That is the posture of the devil himself. The Lord has been impressing upon me the importance of our obedience and avoiding rebellion. If we want to be used by God, in a significant way, we must take the same stance towards rebellion that He takes towards it.

This is a tough topic to talk about and for people to take in. I said in a previous chapter that as we move forward in time, towards the end of time, we will see the full outworking of sin and rebellion in the world around us. They will reach their climax before all things are settled once and for all. As I watch the news weekly, that scenario is playing out.

When it comes to delegated authority, we have to be very, very careful about our attitudes and our opinions on the matter. We also need to guard our speech about it. As I look forward, to the coming revival, I realize that the eyes of the world are going to be on us. They will be sizing us up to see if we walk the talk. I am not as concerned with the eyes of the world as I am with representing our King well. We cannot represent our King well while advocating or participating in rebellion at the same time.

This topic, as with many other subjects in Christianity, has unhealthy positions on either side of the issue. On the one hand, if we are mistaken in our views on this topic, then we align ourselves with rebellion and place ourselves in an anti-Christ position, which is a very dangerous place to be. On the other end of the pendulum, we can find ourselves in positions of blind obedience and end up in deception. I was in blind obedience, but thankfully I was not in deception to the Lord. So maybe a note of clarity is needed. I am referring here to the kind of blind obedience that would be cult-like, where we start believing "another gospel" because we are deceived, and so we have blind obedience to a heretic, for example. The enemy of our souls loves to play on both boundaries, so we must understand what God says about delegated authority and where the boundaries are. It has to be clear in our thought, and uncompromising. And it can never change based on how we're treated. That is not a qualifier.

As we have seen already, there are some tough and severe lessons in the Bible about interacting with delegated authority, and we have been conditioned, as Americans especially, to have this attitude of independence, and a posture that we can do whatever we want. On the one hand, we have a representative form of government, and so the general idea behind it is that it exists to serve the people, and if we don't like what the government does then we are free to rebel and overthrow it. On the other hand, many view America as God's chosen nation, and so they follow blindly along under the guise that the American government makes the best decisions or is a superior authority. I am not so sure that we are allowed to have either position as children of God and members of the Kingdom of God. Unlike America, the Kingdom of God is not a democracy, nor is it a representative form of government. If we could view the throne room of God today, we would not see the American flag behind His right shoulder and the Christian flag behind His left shoulder. We would maybe see the banner of the Lord if there are any banners at all; perhaps all we would see is the train of His robe.

The Kingdom of God is not subject to popular opinion, voter referendum, or constitutional rights. There are no conventions or delegates. There are no protests, movements, marches, or riots to express injustice, unhappiness, or unrest. Jesus does not take polls to see how we're feeling about one issue or another, and there are no elected officials.

Now it is my opinion that we live in the greatest country that has ever existed on earth. It is the greatest country because it is probably the best choice out of all of the available choices. I say that recognizing some of the horrible atrocities that were committed to both establish this nation and grow it. The consequences of those horrible atrocities are still being reaped. And I hate to say it but matters of the heart cannot be fixed by the government. Righteousness cannot be legislated. So even though I think it may be the best country, it is not the answer to the sickness of sin. Only the Kingdom of God provides those answers.

The ideas and principles of an American democratic government are not the ideas and principles of the Kingdom of God. In some cases, the American ideals have been inspired by principles of the Kingdom of God, which is why we see so many attempts to purge those principles from our way of life. However, we cannot bring the American ideal to bear, reason about it, and then impose it on the Kingdom. It does not work that way. This is why I talked about reasoning earlier in this book. We read about authority issues in the Bible, and then we attempt to mold what we see in the text to fit what we are comfortable with in our American view of life. I once heard Bill Johnson say words to the effect of, "As people study great subjects of Scripture, they come to the subjects with their definition and then they allow their definition to re-define what the Bible says." He used *love* as an example. We conceptualize in our mind, in our reasoning, what love is, and then try and apply that reasoning to the Bible. That is an absolute violation of Scripture. The Bible defines the topic of love. God is love. If we want to know love, then know God. We should take what the Bible says about love and allow it to form our perspective. That's the proper order.

Likewise, the Bible defines the topic of authority. We don't get to come up with our feel-good definition and then redefine what the Bible says. **We cannot distort the Word of God to fit a lifestyle that makes us feel good.** There is judgment for rebellious decisions that are decisions against Christ. Jesus is the Word of God. So when we formulate ideas and opinions, when we reason them out, especially on the topic of authority, if our reasoning is misguided, then we're not just transgressing God's definition of authority, we are transgressing against God Himself. Satan's rebellion was not just him running contrary to God's idea of what should be. Satan's rebellion was an affront to the very character and being of God because God is authority. Authority does not exist without Him, and to trample on His authority is to assault God in His person and His position.

Let's look at more Scripture. I am starting in Romans 12 to give literary context to what we will read. The subheading in my Bible before verse 9 is "Marks of a True Christian"; let's keep that in mind as we read.

> Let love be genuine. Abhor what is evil; hold fast to what is good. Love one another with brotherly affection. Outdo one another in showing honor. Don't be slothful in zeal, be fervent in spirit, serve the Lord. Rejoice in hope, be patient in tribulation, be constant in prayer. Contribute to the needs of the saints and seek to show hospitality. Bless those who persecute you; bless and don't curse them. Rejoice with those who rejoice, weep with those who weep. Live in harmony with one another. Don't be haughty, but associate with the lowly. Never be wise in your sight. Repay no one evil for evil, but give thought to do what is honorable in the sight of all. If possible, so far as it depends on you, live peaceably with all. Beloved, never avenge yourselves, but leave it to the wrath of God, for it is written, "Vengeance is mine, I will repay, says the Lord." To the contrary, "if your enemy is hungry, feed him; if he is thirsty, give him something to drink; for by so doing you will heap burning coals on his head." Don't be overcome by evil, but overcome evil with good.

-Romans 12:9-21

Let every person be subject to the governing authorities. For there is no authority except from God, and those that exist have been instituted by God. Therefore whoever resists the authorities resists what God has appointed, and those who resist will incur judgment. For rulers are not a terror to good conduct, but to bad. Would you have no fear of the one who is in authority? Then do what is good, and you will receive his approval, for he is God's servant for your good. But if you do wrong, be afraid, for he does not bear the sword in vain. For he is the servant of God, an avenger who carries out God's wrath on the wrongdoer. Therefore one must be in subjection, not only to avoid God's wrath but also for the sake of conscience. For because of this you also pay taxes, for the authorities are ministers of God, attending to this very thing. Pay to all what is owed to them: taxes to whom taxes are owed, revenue to whom revenue is owed, respect to whom respect is owed, honor to whom honor is owed.

-Romans 13:1-7

In analyzing this portion of Scripture, the historical and cultural context of it is important to understand. Many scholars believe that the date of the writing of Romans was in the mid to late 50s A.D. (some date it as late as 57 A.D., but most scholars agree on the winter of 54-55 A.D.). In 54 A.D., Emperor Claudius died, and Nero took over. Early in his reign Nero was known for practicing every kind of obscenity. There was a man named Tacitus (56-118) who was a Roman senator and historian. He wrote two major works, *The Annals* and *The Histories*, both of which have survived history. Tacitus described Rome during the rule of Nero as "the City where all degraded and shameful practices collect from all over and become vogue." Nero openly raped vestigial virgins and he publicly married a boy named *Sporus*. Nero was ousted in A.D. 68 by a rebellion, and rather than face execution, he committed suicide. This is the historical and cultural context of Romans, and Paul writes this discourse through chapters 12 & 13, which talks about the character traits of being a Christian in the midst of it.

One of those traits of a true Christian is being subject to delegated authority. If anyone had a reason to write something about being disobedient to evil authorities, it was Paul. But he did not. Instead, he encouraged submission and discouraged rebellion. We have to make up in our minds ahead of time that we are going to be submitted to authority. All authority comes from God. **To rebel against a delegated authority is to rebel against God.**

Now, this is where we like to let our reasoning take over. As I write these words, we are in the middle of a pandemic in the United States. This situation has pushed us squarely into the debate about the Church and submission to authority. Sadly, many of the believers out there are expressing just how ignorant they are about the Scriptures, and how rebellious their hearts are.

Recently I saw on social media a ten-minute word-of-the-day from a seasoned minister of the Gospel. This man has been around, and in, the ministry for a long time. He has spoken in my church. Like me, he was asked by several people who follow him online to address whether or not it is time for the church to enter into civil disobedience over the restrictions in place in the U.S. because of the pandemic; specifically regarding the prohibition of having church services in person. He started his broadcast by mentioning that a judge in Oregon had struck down its governor's coronavirus restrictions as null and void.

A group of pastors filed a lawsuit against their governor over the restrictions in Oregon, particularly when it came to barring churches from meeting in person. My understanding is that in Oregon, when the governor puts a restriction in place, like these pandemic restrictions, they must be approved by the state legislature within 28 days according to that state's law. I guess she did not follow that law with her restrictions and so the judge struck them down for that reason. The judge viewed the restrictions against churches meeting to be unconstitutional as well.

As an aside, I believe this was the right way for these pastors to handle this situation. They did not rebel against the governor's order, but instead, they used the system available at their disposal to file suit and see her order overturned. While they awaited the verdict, they complied with the unjust restriction. I submit to you that was the best way to handle the situation in their circumstance. They did not run afoul of God's expectations of obedience to delegated authority, and yet they were also vindicated and successful in court getting her restriction overturned legally. That is biblical order.

So, the question came to this pastor who was teaching online, "What does God have to say about submitting to authority based on Romans 13?" This pastor read Romans 13, verses 1-4, and then asked this question, "So biblically, when is civil disobedience okay?" His response, frankly, astounded me.

He said the answer begins with the fact that the Apostle Paul was writing specifically to the Christian church, under the rule of Rome, in the first century, which means that Romans 13 was "not intended to apply to every situation, under every government, in every age to come." He went on to say,

> At the time that Paul wrote, Rome was the best, the most just government that had yet existed on earth. Rome had established the *pax romana*, the peace of Rome, that had made trade possible all over the Mediterranean basin. Rome built roads where there had been none and made travel safe on the sea. All of that allowed commerce to thrive. Everybody prospered because the Roman government kept the bad guys at bay. It was a just enough government, that if you behaved yourself, if you paid your taxes, if you didn't kill anybody, and you carried yourself as an honest subject of the empire, then you didn't have anything to worry about.

He continued that if we hold that Romans 13 applies to everyone for all time, then logically we are forced to conclude that very evil rulers also received their authority from God. He mentioned several evil notables like Hitler, Stalin, and Kim Jung Un, and his conclusion was obvious: that those men's authority cannot possibly be from God because of how evil they were. He then assures his viewers that Paul was specifically writing about those rulers, at that time, specifically in that place. His further conclusion is that all authority since then must be judged based on God's principles and God's laws. He also says that if an authority is established by God, then the fruit of their governing will show it, making it obvious.

The conclusion I surmise then, from his analysis is, if the fruit of their governing is not obvious, then we are under no obligation to obey because, in his view, they are not a legitimate authority. If that's true, then that's a problem for us in America, because our government's fruit demonstrates, most of the time, that they're not doing a good job and the fruit of their governing is usually anti-biblical. Again, that's my conclusion of his analysis theory. But can I ask a question at this juncture? What nation on earth has the fruit, based on their governing, that they are established by God? The last time I surveyed the situation, I did not find any Christian nation utopias out there.

As kindly as I can say it, I don't think that I have ever heard a worse biblical and cultural exposition of Romans 13 than I did watching that video. Let's say this speaker is right and Paul was only writing about the rulers of that time. Then Paul was still advocating submission and obedience to an absolute tyrant who tortured Christians, raped women, and was openly homosexual!! On the cultural level, Rome may have established the *pax romana*, but to say that Rome was the justest government that had existed on earth up until that time is ridiculous. What about all the righteous kings in the Old Testament who followed the Lord, and who caused Israel to follow the Lord during their reigns? They, too, prospered economically and had peace with their enemies. Why? Because the Lord caused it to be so. The idea that Rome was the first empire to be just and prosperous is absurd. Rome burned and killed Christians by the thousands. Nero, who was emperor when Paul wrote his letter to the Romans, covered Christians in oil, tied them to posts in his garden, and set them on fire to use them as human lanterns. He fed Christian men, women, and children to the lions in the Coliseum, for sport. That was the most just government in existence?

Furthermore, I did not know there was a "too evil" exemption clause to Scripture. What this ministry leader has asserted in his teaching is that the principle in Romans 13 only applies to that first-century church because if it were generally applied, when we get to someone who is super evil, it puts us in the tough position of having to acknowledge that maybe their authority came from God, too. But that offends our way of thinking, so instead, we reason it out and limit the Scriptures. Then we can exempt the really bad people in history from the delegated authority principle, saying they didn't get their authority from God, because of course, we have to defend God and His principles. Such terrible, open-ended analysis is reckless and dangerous. Theology like this leaves us to selectively pick the Scripture verses we like to follow and throw out the others we don't; we judge who we are to obey, and willfully disregard anyone we don't judge as worthy of our obedience. And what do we do with the rest of Romans if we follow this same pattern of biblical analysis? Is the rest of Romans only applicable to that church at that time or is this restriction only applied to chapter 13? And if it is, how does he know that, and who decides what parts are applicable and what's not applicable, being as there is no scriptural support for that idea whatsoever?

I guess in his view, Hitler was worse than King Ahab; Stalin was worse than King Jeroboam, and Kim Jung Un was worse than King Manasseh. Or maybe those Old Testament kings did not get their authority from God either? Wrong! They got their authority to be king from God just like every other delegated authority that has ever existed.

I can see why someone would hypothesize such a thing; I just don't see Scripture to support it. It is deception! The principle of Romans 13 is to be submitted to authority. Period. It applies to all people, not just Christians, at all times, in all circumstances, except, in those specific instances where the Bible sanctions civil disobedience (which I will cover in the next chapter). We don't get to choose the circumstances under which civil disobedience is allowed. It's already been demonstrated for us in the Book.

The Evil Ruler/Leader

On its face, the idea that an evil leader does not get their authority from God and is somehow a counterfeit authority is intriguing. So, let's expound on that idea and see if there is anything to this "evil people" exemption. I believe I can prove that the level of good or evil a ruler exhibits has nothing to do with whether their authority was obtained from God or not.

As I wrote in chapter 2, God naturally has all authority. Why? Because He is the Creator. No one gave Him His authority and He did not receive His authority from any source other than Himself. Every other authority in existence is delegated. If there is an authority in existence, it has received its authority from God. How do I know? I know because there is no other source of authority from which to get authority. There is no "good and evil" clause on that.

How God manages this issue is God gives and holds people accountable. That is how He operates. It has not changed since the beginning of time. Why? Because God never changes. If we accept the theory that He only gives authority to good rulers, we begin to see contradictions about leadership throughout the Scripture.

First, define *good* for me. What is good? What is the threshold of a good ruler that would warrant a conclusion their authority came from God versus someone else? Where does the good/evil line lie? If they start good and then they go bad (e.g., Solomon) did their authority come from God at first, and then not so much later? Jesus told the rich young ruler that no one was good but God. If we follow this good versus evil theory about authority, does it apply to other things God gives, like gifts too? I mean, why not? Makes sense, right? God only gives gifts to those people who are going to be good. For everyone else, there is no way their gifting comes from God. Really? Would that argument hold up to scrutiny? Of course, it would not, it's a ridiculous notion. We can see that God gifts people, just like He gives them authority. What they do with it, is up to them.

Have you ever known a gifted person that did not serve the Lord? Of course, there are thousands of them cranking out very gifted worldly music all the time. Have you ever known a gifted person that served the Lord and then fell? I have. Their gifting does not go away though, does it? No, it doesn't. Sadly, it continues to function, and most often, people who have fallen are deceived into believing they haven't fallen because their gift continues to function. Thus, they confuse gifting and calling with godly approval and anointing.

The sad fact is some people use their gifting or authority, or both, for good or great good; and some people use it for evil, and yes, great and terrible evil. But God operates the same, and He is not threatened by their behavior. He does not explain Himself or defend His program. He waits. He waits until the day of accountability and judgment. Explain to me why He allowed some evil kings to rule for 40 or 50 years, and others 3 months? You cannot. Why? Because it's part of the mystery of God, and He did not tell us, and He does not owe us an explanation. He does not have to explain every authority issue to us so that we are comfortable with His decisions. He is not subject to us; we are subject to Him.

Now, listen very carefully to what dropped in my spirit while I was writing on this. God created man, and set him in the garden, and gave him what? (Christianity 101 again. Everyone knows this.) God gave man His authority. Why? So man could rule and have dominion and represent God as a delegated authority on the earth. What happened next? Satan stole that authority. So here's the question: did God then revoke the authority from Satan when he stole it? The answer is, no, He did not. Not for thousands of years until Jesus Christ came. So, here's the conclusion. Satan's authority on the earth, during that time, from the fall in the Garden, until the death and Resurrection of Jesus, came from God. That means Satan had God's authority over the earth for around 4,000 years. I know we hate how that sounds, but we know this is factual from Scripture. It in no way means that God was consenting to how Satan used that authority. It in no way means God was pleased with the situation, but it does not change the fact that that is what occurred. As I wrote earlier, Satan offered the authority he had to Jesus during His temptation.

> The devil led him up to a high place and showed him in an instant all the kingdoms of the world. And he said to him, "I will give you all their authority and splendor; it has been given to me, and I can give it to anyone I want to. If you worship me, it will all be yours."
>
> -Luke 4:5-7

There it is, right in the Gospels. Satan's authority had been given to him, that authority originated from God, and Satan could delegate it to others. Now, we know that God did not give it to him directly, and God would not have given it to him directly, but that does not change the fact that it came from God nonetheless because man was swindled out of it. Satan often speaks in twisted half-truths as he does in this passage, because the whole truth is that he stole the authority from man through deceit; it wasn't given to him. But, if the only source of delegated authority is intrinsic authority, then our only conclusion is Satan's authority came from God, stolen or not. There is no way around it. And that authority remained with Satan for thousands of years.

Now here, in the temptation of Jesus, Satan is offering to the Lord the same path he chose to take, the shortcut to the throne so-to-speak. Jesus, making the right decision, refuses to be Satan's delegated authority and circumvent His process of promotion, by choosing instead to be submitted to God's will, plan and purpose, so that He can take back the authority given by God and lost by man; only to eventually give it right back to mankind who forfeited it in the first place.

So if Satan can get his authority from God, are you telling me there is a problem with concluding that Hitler's or Stalin's authority came from God? They are worse than Satan? Since when? This pastor from the video said that Hitler killed 14 million people, therefore he could not possibly have received his authority from God. Okay, how many has the devil murdered through spinning up anger, division, warfare, and evil? Probably in the billions. Hitler, as evil as he was, has nothing on the devil. And I am not making light of what Hitler did; it is one of the biggest travesties of human history, but we don't get to change how the Kingdom of God operates because it does not mesh well with our personal theological paradigms that are influenced by what we see man do.

See the problem here is, again, our reasoning. It is like Christians have a pass on being dumb. We fall for such stupid, stupid analysis of things. I am sorry if that offends, but why do we fall for this garbage? We fall for it because, #1, we don't know the Word. People don't know the Word of God, and they react out of their flesh. "My people perish for a lack of knowledge," the Lord said in Hosea 4:6. They react stupidly, they say dumb things, and they believe dumb things. And I am not special, but I am thankful to God that I am not deceived and that I do my best to know the Word. But because we don't know the Word, our thinking is distorted, and it gives the opportunity for the devil to twist the truth.

We also think that because of injustice, God is somehow boxed into a corner. God did not revoke Satan's authority when he stole it from man, instead, He put into action the coming of His Son who would take back authority by living a sinless life and being an atonement for all sin for all time. See, God is big enough that He plays by His own rules. He binds Himself to His own Word. He does not get baited into quick responses to satisfy the immediate cry of injustice. He will satisfy all injustice, but it will be in a long-term way, in the most permanent way, and in a way that brings Him the most glory. It will never be in the way that pacifies human beings and their opinion of Him or His decisions in the short-term so that they say something flowery about Him on their social media accounts.

The next thing this pastor did, which is a common failure on the part of American Christians everywhere, was to move on to a discussion of the American way of life, democracy, our rights as citizens, how our government officials are elected to do our bidding, etc. Thus, blurring the lines between being an American citizen and being a citizen of the Kingdom. Those are two entirely different things. One of the things this pastor said was that when these officials don't do our bidding, then we must disobey, and we must hold them accountable. I agree with the second part. He went on to say that God's laws supersede man's laws. I agree with that. And when man's laws cause us to or would cause us to, violate God's laws, we must not obey. I agree with that. He referenced Acts 5 as an example, when Peter and John are told not to preach in Jesus' name, and they refuse. I am glad he used that example because that is one of the instances where the Bible sanctions rebellion to delegated authority. But then he used a not-so-good example to illustrate how we must rebel against the authorities. He quoted this passage:

> Let us hold fast the confession of our hope without wavering, for He who promised is faithful. And let us consider one another in order to stir up love and good works, not forsaking the assembling of ourselves together, as is the manner of some, but exhorting one another, and so much the more as you see the Day approaching.
> -Hebrews 10:23-25

So, he says that verse is a command from God to gather together in a community, and what these governing authorities are doing by restricting church services because of a pandemic is causing us to disobey God's clear commands. I don't know that I can swallow that without further discussion, because there's more to that than this explanation he's given.

First, what if our response was to use his response to Romans 13? Why can't I say that this passage from Hebrews was only written to that church, at that time, under those specific circumstances and was not intended to apply to all people, for all time, under all circumstances? See what happens when we step out onto the slippery slope? There's no end to where the slide stops. No, Hebrews 10 applies to all of us today, just as much as Romans 13, and the rest of God's Word for that matter.

But this instruction was not telling the church that God was commanding them to come together. This was advice and counsel, good and godly advice and counsel, from a father in the faith to a group of Christians that were dealing with issues of apostasy. *Hebrews* is written to Christian Jews who were falling away from the faith, turning their back on their belief in Jesus, and backsliding. The whole book is filled with warnings about falling away and neglecting their salvation. So, the advice and counsel of this leader of the early church who wrote this book was, don't neglect to gather yourselves together so we can stay built up in the faith. It had nothing to do with government suppression, a health crisis, or having church in secret as part of being civilly disobedient.

As an aside, I would advocate the same advice to us today as the author of Hebrews gave to his readers. I hate when I hear people say they don't hate God, they just hate the church, or that they are Christians, yet they just don't go to church. The recipe for success in the Christian life—part of the recipe—is keeping yourself in church and staying in community with God's people.

Lastly, this pastor rounds out his discussion of the issues at hand with a reading of parts of the U.S. Constitution, and he goes on a bit of a speech about rights as Americans. So here, for me, is when this whole thing gets blurred, and it is just one terrible conclusion after another. And for the sake of time, I just want to cut to the chase.

The first thing I will say is this. If you are a believer, you are a citizen of the Kingdom of God first and you are subject to the King of kings. I don't care what the U.S. Constitution says we have the right to do. We must be submitted to the Lord. If the Constitution grants us some other liberty, we need to ensure that liberty does not run afoul of the Kingdom of God. For example, it has been ruled that the constitutional right of women is to have an abortion. Well, I am sorry, that runs afoul of the Kingdom of God, so I could care less what the Constitution says about it. Now, so it is clear, I don't have a problem with the Constitution, nor being an American. I am very grateful to be an American, but those rights are secondary and subservient to my duty as a citizen of the Kingdom.

We also err when we begin to evaluate whether the authorities we are faced with are worthy of being an authority. We kind of put them through this litmus test. Am I under them? Are they someone I respect? Do they deserve to be over me? Do they belong to my political party? Are they Christian? Do I agree with what they are saying? None of those questions are relevant to our obligation to be submitted and obedient. We reason that we should support the good authorities and oppose the bad; from our perspective, that's what God would want us to do after all. We further reason that God would only use a good authority and would not use a bad authority, and He certainly would never have us submit to evil authority. If an authority is mistreating us or being unjust with us, God would not want us to feel bad, so we are free from having to be submitted. All of that reasoning is flawed.

The first problem with that line of thinking is that we reason that we are adequately equipped to determine what makes a good authority and what makes a bad authority and who should even be an authority. The second problem is believing that is a relevant discussion to have before we determine our submission and obedience. Even in that situation, we are incapable because God sees from an eternal perspective and we see from a finite perspective. We are not qualified to make those decisions, and when we do, we suppose ourselves to be on the same level of counsel as God. How foolish, prideful, and deceitful! And let me save you time on whether there is a qualifier for whether or not we are to be submitted to authority; there is not. In those instances, we are bringing to the text our perspective, what makes us feel good, and in doing so we attempt to redefine the Word.

Here is the position of Scripture. There are delegated authorities in the world. We are to be subject (submitted) to them. We are not to resist them. We are to do good and hopefully gain praise from the authorities. We are to pay taxes and revenue to them if they are owed, and we are to render to them respect and honor. If we don't, we bring judgment on ourselves and we are in rebellion towards the ordinance of God. See, we cannot say we obey God and then disregard His delegated authorities. We err if we believe that we can choose between God's intrinsic authority and His delegated authority because there is no authority except from God. To disregard God's delegated authority is to disregard God. 1 Peter 2:13-25,

Be subject for the Lord's sake to every human institution, whether it be to the emperor as supreme, or to governors as sent by him to punish those who do evil and to praise those who do good. For this is the will of God, that by doing good you should put to silence the ignorance of foolish people. Live as people who are free, not using your freedom as a cover-up for evil, but living as servants of God. Honor everyone. Love the brotherhood. Fear God. Honor the emperor. Servants, be subject to your masters with all respect, not only to the good and gentle but also to the unjust. For this is a gracious thing, when, mindful of God, one endures sorrows while suffering unjustly. For what credit is it if, when you sin and are beaten for it, you endure? But if when you do good and suffer for it you endure, this is a gracious thing in the sight of God. For to this you have been called, because Christ also suffered for you, leaving you an example, so that you might follow in his steps. He committed no sin, neither was deceit found in his mouth. When he was reviled, he did not revile in return; when he suffered, he did not threaten, but continued entrusting himself to him who judges justly. He himself bore our sins in his body on the tree, that we might die to sin and live to righteousness. By his wounds you have been healed. For you were straying like sheep, but have now returned to the Shepherd and Overseer of your souls.

-1 Peter 2:13-25

One argument we as pastors hear from people who are rebellious in church is, "Well, I just have to do what God tells me to do" or "I take my instructions from the Lord." Yes, we do have to do what God tells us to do, and as good as that sounds, those kinds of statements are the safest places for a rebel to hide. Used in the context of dishonoring or disobeying authority that we are subjected to, those very statements are self-defeating.

Let me tell you about true leadership. As a leader, when you have to deal with people on tough decisions, when they are saying things like that to you and you know they are rebellious or being deceived, that is a real cross to bear. And a leader who is willing to confront that attitude and attempts to pierce the veil of deception so that the rebellious one can be saved from disaster does not take pleasure in the fact that the person is deceived. When you have to confront someone, it should hurt to do it. There is no pleasure in it. You will not see a true leader reveling at that moment. You will not observe an attitude of "you'll see." Most often you will not see anything from the leader, but you may hear criticism about them. The true leader will not defend himself. Watchman Nee writes that "authority and self-defense are incompatible."[4] God is the vindicator, a true leader will not offer his defense, but will defer to God. What the true leader will do is be in the secret place weeping, pouring out their heart to God to save the person from their deception. The bad part about deception is it is deceiving, and I often wonder what can save a person who is deceived. I know a guy that is practically a paranoid, delusional basket case, but to him, he is the only guy that he can trust. The Lord is his number one defender and as long as he just listens to the Lord, he will be fine. The guy is bound for hell and no one can save him. Apart from the Lord being exceptionally merciful to him and just encountering him in such a way that all of that deception falls off, the guy is going to be lost. But he got to that position by being consistently rebellious, avoiding godly counsel, being unwilling to submit, and being fooled that his encounters with the Lord, while spectacular, were all he needed to make it, and thus his rebellious heart and actions are justified before the Lord.

Let me tell you about statements like, "Well, I just have to do what God tells me to do." God must be true to Himself first. He cannot contradict Himself. Therefore, He cannot contradict His own Word, because He is the Word. Therefore, if we are not in a position of delegated authority, but we are rather a "free spirit," then not only would He not give us instruction contrary to His delegated authority, He cannot. It is not possible. I don't care if someone thinks they heard Him, they did not. Again, this is where reasoning comes into play. People reason that God has given them some exception from His Word because what they are being told to do by a leader does not line up with their feelings on a particular issue. So, they utter statements like "I just have to do what God tells me to do," to try and divert their accountability. I am sorry, that does not work. It is rebellion and a principle of Satan.

Well what if my pastor or leader is wrong you might ask? Do I not have a right to ignore them and follow what I think the Lord is telling me? If what they are telling you to do is not illegal, unethical, or immoral, then no, you don't have a right to be disobedient. We must be submitted and obedient, and leave the results up to God. Listen, if the delegated authority messes up, then God will come to judge. It is not up to us. Watchman Nee says it this way:

> He who resists authority resists God, and those who resist will incur judgment. There is no possibility of rebellion without judgment. The consequence of resisting authority is death. Man has no choice in the matter of authority.[5]

We are not talking about delegated authorities being right or wrong. We are talking about our obligation to authority as Christians. What do we have to do to be in obedience to God? This topic is like forgiveness. If we are wronged by someone else, and it is 100% their fault, and there is a disagreement between us and them, we are still responsible for going to them and asking for forgiveness. Our rebellious nature revolts at such a thought, because after all, it is not our fault. We are in the right. We deserve justification! Not what the Bible says. The point is not who is right or wrong. The point is never who is right and who is wrong. The point is obedience to God. Will you be obedient and go ask for forgiveness even when it's not your fault?

I was recently giving counsel to someone who had some unforgiveness about a situation, who I suppose was innocent of all wrongdoing. And I told them they had the responsibility to go apologize and ask for forgiveness. I also said, after you ask for forgiveness, whatever happens after that is irrelevant. If they accept your apology, great! If they scorn you and tell you to get lost, great! At that point, you have done your duty to God's instruction. You are free and clear of all further responsibility. The outcome is left to God and the other person. You are free.

Authority is the same way. What is your obligation under God's view on authority? We are not responsible for anyone else. I am responsible for myself. You are responsible for yourself. Make sure that you do your obligation under authority, lest you incur judgment. You cannot say to the Lord, "well he made me," or "he was being mean," or "I was right," or "I deserved…". None of those answers matter.

From the time of Adam, God gave authority to man. Notice

that in the initial mandate to man God did not give authority to Adam over other men. He gave him authority over animals. Why? Because man was to be under God's authority. Authority over man would come later. Let's look at a passage from Genesis 9.

> And God blessed Noah and his sons and said to them, "Be fruitful and multiply and fill the earth. The fear of you and the dread of you shall be upon every beast of the earth and upon every bird of the heavens, upon everything that creeps on the ground and all the fish of the sea. Into your hand they are delivered. Every moving thing that lives shall be food for you. And as I gave you the green plants, I give you everything. But you shall not eat flesh with its life, that is, its blood. And for your lifeblood I will require a reckoning: from every beast I will require it and from man. From his fellow man I will require a reckoning for the life of man. Whoever sheds the blood of man, by man shall his blood be shed, for God made man in his own image. And you, be fruitful and multiply, increase greatly on the earth and multiply in it."
>
> -Genesis 9:1-7

This is the first time in Scripture that we see man subjected to man, and ever since then, the authority of governing man has been invested in men. God reaffirmed this practice in the Law. Exodus 22:28, "You shall not revile God, nor curse a ruler of your people." God continued to use men as His delegated authority, without regard to whether they were good or evil. In other words, He did not violate the structure that He set up just because things didn't go well. He stuck with the plan, even going so far as to use wicked kings who were pagan to accomplish His purposes. He went so far as to call them His servants.

> Now I have given all these lands into the hand of Nebuchadnezzar, king of Babylon, my servant, and I have given him also the beasts of the field to serve him.
>
> -Jeremiah 27:6

> Thus says the Lord to his anointed, to Cyrus, whose right hand I have grasped, to subdue nations before him and to loose the belts of kings, to open doors before him that gates may not be closed: "I will go before you and level the exalted places, I will break in pieces the doors of bronze and cut through the bars of iron, I will give you the treasures of darkness and the hoards in secret places, that you may know that it is I, the Lord, the God of Israel, who call you by your name."
>
> -Isaiah 45:1-3 (ESV)

So even evil kings were the servant of the Lord, according to God's mouth.

Now right up through the NT, the principle of submitting to authority is found. Jesus was subject to governing authorities and the high priest. He paid taxes and taught men to render to Caesar what was Caesar's. So, the question is not whether we should be submitted and obey delegated authority. The question is, "do we recognize them as God's authority?" Good or bad, right or wrong, will we recognize authority for what it is? See it would be great if we only had to honor the good ones, or if there was some litmus test to put them through before we decided against submitting and obeying, but there is not.

In Jude, verse 9, we see an account of an interaction between Michael the archangel and Satan, disputing about the body of Moses. I think this story is interesting as it relates to the discussion of authority. It's widely held that Satan, before his fall, was the highest order of created beings. In Ezekiel 28:12, he is called "the model of perfection, full of wisdom and perfect in beauty." When he fell, we know he took a third of the host of heaven with him, so he was likely the highest angel, in rank, that was created. So at that time, before his fall, Michael would have been under Satan's authority and command. Now in Jude 9, we see that even Michael did not enter into reviling or rebellion when dealing with Satan even though he was a fallen being, he said "The Lord rebuke you." So even though Satan is fallen, Michael did not take a position of superiority and pride and try and rebuke the devil. He stayed low and humble, reflecting the values of the Kingdom to which he belongs.

Aside from that example, we have David and his interactions with Saul. What a powerful study on submission to authority is the life of David. I could probably write a book on authority using nothing but the life of David. All I will say in brief is that Saul tried to kill David multiple times. David was chosen by God to be the next king of Israel, and God had even torn the kingdom away from Saul by the mouth of the prophet Samuel, yet David would not lift a finger to advance his agenda or to kill the man of God who had previously been anointed king.

What a tremendous risk God has taken in using delegated authority. This is what we have to remember. If authorities are wrong, if they are evil, if they abuse their power, it is not for us to take it upon ourselves to deal with it. God alone is responsible for them. Did He know what they would do with authority before He ever put the first authority in place? Yes, He did, and He did it anyway. Don't forget what I said earlier, God must be true to Himself first. Therefore, if He put a delegated authority in place, then He is bound by Himself to honor that authority until He decides to revoke their authority. But He is the only one who gets to make that decision, and that is God's call and not ours. It does not mean that they are not accountable, and it does not mean that He sanctions everything they do, but it does mean that we are called upon to recognize them as an authority and to be submitted to them.

This is the final point I want to offer to give you some perspective on this. When we are submitted and obedient to delegated authority, we are not submitting and being obedient to the person, we are being submitted and obedient to their position and God's authority on their life. It's not a personality test or a popularity contest. We have to choose to be submitted and obedient because of what they are, not who they are. And what they are is God's delegated authority, therefore we must do what is right before the Lord regarding them and not what we feel like doing. To do otherwise is to enter into rebellion and advocate the principles of the kingdom of darkness, because authority, and more importantly, submission to authority, is a paramount aspect of our lives. God WILL NOT partner with a rebellious people. He can't. He is restricted by His nature from doing so. You see, God must remain true to Himself above everything else, and in everything that He does. So to partner with rebellion would be a violation against Himself, and He cannot do that. Rebellion, as we saw in a previous chapter, is a principle of Satan, it's the worship of the devil, and God can have no part of rebellion. The reality of that can be staggering because rebellion is in our nature and we engage in it all of the time. We probably would not call it rebellion and we certainly would not like it pointed out to us as such, but in its nature, that's exactly what it is. It affects everything we do. In everything you do, be submitted. It's one of the only pieces of solid advice I would stake my life on.

11
THE LESSON OF KING JOSIAH

And like unto him was there no king before him, that turned to the Lord with all his heart, and with all his soul, and with all his might, according to all the law of Moses; neither after him arose there any like him.
-2 Kings 23:25

Sometimes we can be so strong for God in a matter, that we end up opposing Him. That's exactly what happened to a young lady from Kentucky. Kim Davis was the Clerk of Rowan County, Kentucky, and part of her job was to issue marriage licenses. The U.S. Supreme Court recognized a constitutional right to same-sex marriage in *Obergefell v. Hodges* in 2015. Obviously, from the Christian viewpoint and worldview, same-sex marriage is both a sin and an abomination to God, but the Supreme Court made it the law of the land whether we like it or not.

Enter Kim Davis, who, due to her Christian beliefs, refused to follow the orders of her employers, the Governor of Kentucky, and several courts of law, and issue same-sex marriage licenses. She was widely championed by social conservatives and lauded by prominent pastors and leaders throughout the Christian church in America. I was not one of those pastors.

While I stand opposed to same-sex marriage and everything it represents, I cannot endorse rebellion, and Kim Davis was rebellious in every definition of the word. I understand her beliefs and I support them, but the minute she sacrifices one principle of God (obedience to authority) for another principle of God (marriage between a man and a woman) she's entered into rebellion. God does not fight that way. If you want your sin so much that you make it federal law for yourself, then God lets you have that sin. The Bible says He gives you the desire of your heart (Psalm 37:4). Most people never conceive of the fact that those can be bad desires, too. You see, God is unwilling to make anyone do anything; He lets you have exactly what you want to have. Some people want to spend eternity without Jesus, and God will give them exactly what they want. If you want more of Him, He gives it to you. If you want more of sin, He gives you over to that, too.

And Kim became so strong for God in the matter of marriage, that she ended up opposing God in the matter of submission to authority. God is not honored by that. God does not receive glory through that. God would have no part of that. In the end, Kim was sued, and she lost her case and her job as county clerk. She appealed to the Supreme Court and lost there, too. She ended up proving nothing and she didn't stop anything. Now she may sleep better at night knowing she took a stand, but I would submit that her motives were ill-placed.

The right thing for her to do was to resign. She could have made a public statement. She could have spelled out her Christian convictions, been a great Christian example, given glory to God, honored her employers, bosses, authorities, and courts, and sacrificed her job in the name of Christianity, but she didn't. Instead, she was a bad example in the way she spelled out her Christian convictions, and she lost everything in a dishonorable way. She didn't bring any glory to God with her actions and all she did was solidify in the minds of countless Americans that Christians are bigots. Instead of displaying the tough love of God in holding to a standard of righteousness, she lost that ability by being defiant.

And while the church at large was cheering her on, I was screaming rebellion! This is another thing Christians do, they enter into rebellion to justify something that is supposedly Christian-based, and they truly believe they are honoring God. He is not honored by sin. Kim was not asked to murder the innocent, worship other gods, or do anything illegal, unethical, or immoral. Now critics may pounce and say that issuing a same-sex marriage license is immoral. I say it is not. Immorality is in the act of coming together in same-sex marriage. If anyone is to blame, it is the officiant overseeing the union in same-sex marriage and the participants of the ceremony getting "married". There may come a day when the government mandates that we pastors perform same-sex marriages or be charged with hate crimes. I am prepared to go to jail for that and in that instance; I will rebel, because at that point I would be being asked to do something immoral and it will be my duty to disobey. That would be a scripturally justified rebellion. But we have to navigate these decisions very carefully and with much wisdom and discernment because it's far too easy to end up on the wrong side of the line, especially when we think we're justified by our Christian beliefs.

Just because someone issues a license to be married doesn't mean that license will ever be used. And as the Courts ruled, they in effect said the same. While they acknowledged her sincerely held religious beliefs, she was not the person getting married. I felt all through the situation, the right move was to resign, and maybe even be very vocal about the reason on the way out, but becoming strong for God by rebelling against authority, I can't sanction. And just so you don't think I'm crazy, we see this principle borne out by Scripture.

I knew I could not write this book without talking about one of my favorite characters of the Old Testament, King Josiah. His story holds fascinating similarities to an issue that I see that plagues the modern church. As I have tried to make clear throughout this book, as Christians we have a duty and an obligation to the Lord, and His delegated authorities, to be obedient and submitted. Obedience should be our default mode. Submission and going low should be staples of our character. As I will point out in the next chapter, Jesus did nothing of His own initiative, and we should do likewise. He is, after all, the ultimate example for us.

But invariably, I meet Christians all the time, whose behavior demonstrates to me, that being submitted is the last thing on their minds. Their goals are usually to accomplish something for Jesus, to walk in some ministry, to start using their gift, to save the world through preaching, etc., etc. But I am always amazed at their lack of wanting to be submitted, disciplined, and walking in obedience. And most of the time, their attitude about being submitted is that they cannot because they have to be about the Lord's work, or what they think He has called them to. The very danger of not being submitted is doing your own thing—this is called iniquity and rebellion—and justifying it as the Lord's work. And I want to use King Josiah's life to drive this point home.

I am going to start by talking about King Manasseh, not

because he has anything to do with the authority conversation, but because I want to paint a spectrum for you and lay out where he is on the spectrum compared to Josiah, his grandson, who will provide our lesson on authority.

Manasseh was twelve years old when he became king, and he reigned fifty-five years in Jerusalem. His mother's name was Hephzibah. And he did evil in the sight of the Lord, according to the abominations of the nations whom the Lord had cast out before the children of Israel. For he rebuilt the high places which Hezekiah his father had destroyed; he raised up altars for Baal, and made a wooden image, as Ahab king of Israel had done; and he worshiped all the host of heaven and served them. He also built altars in the house of the Lord, of which the Lord had said, "In Jerusalem I will put My name." And he built altars for all the host of heaven in the two courts of the house of the Lord. Also he made his son pass through the fire, practiced soothsaying, used witchcraft, and consulted spiritists and mediums. He did much evil in the sight of the Lord, to provoke Him to anger. He even set a carved image of Asherah that he had made, in the house of which the Lord had said to David and to Solomon his son, "In this house and in Jerusalem, which I have chosen out of all the tribes of Israel, I will put My name forever; and I will not make the feet of Israel wander anymore from the land which I gave their fathers—only if they are careful to do according to all that I have commanded them, and according to all the law that My servant Moses commanded them." But they paid no attention, and Manasseh seduced them to do more evil than the nations whom the Lord had destroyed before the children of Israel. And the Lord spoke by His servants the prophets, saying, "Because Manasseh king of Judah has done these abominations (he has acted more wickedly than all the Amorites who were before him, and has also made Judah sin with his idols), therefore thus says the Lord God of Israel: 'Behold, I am bringing such calamity upon Jerusalem and Judah, that whoever hears of it, both his ears will tingle. And I will stretch over Jerusalem the measuring line of Samaria and the plummet of the house of Ahab; I will wipe Jerusalem as one wipes a dish, wiping it and turning it upside down. So I will forsake the remnant of My inheritance and deliver them into the hand of their enemies; and they shall become victims of plunder to all their enemies, because they have done evil in My sight, and have provoked Me to anger since the day their fathers came out of Egypt, even to this day.'" Moreover Manasseh shed very much innocent blood, till he had filled Jerusalem from one end to another, besides his sin by which he made Judah sin, in doing evil in the sight of the Lord.

-2 Kings 21:1-16

What a swell guy, right? He's the epitome of an evil king. He received his authority from the Lord though, did he not? Interestingly enough, the Bible says Manasseh repented in 2 Chronicles 33. The Assyrians took him captive to Babylon. He repented and the Lord restored him, but it was not enough to keep God from His wrath. So just like with the Israelites, the saying "I'm sorry" part was good, but it did not negate the judgment. Manasseh's son Amon only reigned two years, and he was just as bad as his father. I guess the Lord was not going to tolerate that again.□□□□□

So, in this environment, Josiah becomes king.

Josiah was eight years old when he became king, and he reigned thirty-one years in Jerusalem. His mother's name was Jedidah the daughter of Adaiah of Bozkath. And he did what was right in the sight of the Lord, and walked in

all the ways of his father David; he did not turn aside to the
right hand or to the left.

-2 Kings 22:1-2

Josiah begins to rule at age eight. Second Chronicles tells us
that at age 16, Josiah began to seek God. At 20, he begins to
make reforms and tear down idols and altars to false gods. He
sets about completely undoing what his father and grandfather
had done. At 26, he commands that the temple be restored, and
Hilkiah finds the Book of the Law. Interestingly, Josiah began to
make these reforms out of his seeking of the Lord. He does not
know what is in the book of the covenant until now. When he
finds out, Josiah is overcome with grief, and he sends his priests
and scribes to a prophetess, Huldah, to hear what the Lord says.

Then she said to them, "Thus says the Lord God of Israel,
'Tell the man who sent you to Me, "Thus says the Lord:
'Behold, I will bring calamity on this place and on its
inhabitants—all the words of the book which the king of
Judah has read— because they have forsaken Me and
burned incense to other gods, that they might provoke Me
to anger with all the works of their hands. Therefore My
wrath shall be aroused against this place and shall not be
quenched.'"" But as for the king of Judah, who sent you to
inquire of the Lord, in this manner you shall speak to him,
'Thus says the Lord God of Israel: "Concerning the words
which you have heard—because your heart was tender, and
you humbled yourself before the Lord when you heard
what I spoke against this place and against its inhabitants,
that they would become a desolation and a curse, and you
tore your clothes and wept before Me, I also have heard
you," says the Lord. "Surely, therefore, I will gather you to
your fathers, and you shall be gathered to your grave in
peace; and your eyes shall not see all the calamity which I

will bring on this place."''' So they brought back word to the king.

-2 Kings 22:15-20

In chapter 23 of Second Kings, Josiah restores true worship. Verses 15-18 record a fulfillment of prophecy that we need to examine,

> Moreover the altar that was at Bethel, and the high place which Jeroboam the son of Nebat, who made Israel sin, had made, both that altar and the high place he broke down; and he burned the high place and crushed it to powder, and burned the wooden image. As Josiah turned, he saw the tombs that were there on the mountain. And he sent and took the bones out of the tombs and burned them on the altar, and defiled it according to the word of the Lord which the man of God proclaimed, who proclaimed these words. Then he said, "What gravestone is this that I see?" So the men of the city told him, "It is the tomb of the man of God who came from Judah and proclaimed these things which you have done against the altar of Bethel."
>
> -2 Kings 23:15-18

In 1 Kings 11, the Bible records the rebellion of Jeroboam. In 1 Kings 12, Rehoboam and Jeroboam, the sons of Solomon, are fighting over the throne and Jeroboam is successful in ruling all of Israel except the tribe of Judah, who pledge their allegiance to Rehoboam.

Jeroboam sets up an altar at Bethel, creates two golden calves as the gods for Israel, and installs false priests for worship. Notice his rebellion led immediately to worship of other gods (i.e., Satan).

In 1 Kings 13, a prophet who is unnamed comes to Bethel from Judah, and this is what he prophesies:

> And behold, a man of God went from Judah to Bethel by the word of the Lord, and Jeroboam stood by the altar to burn incense. Then he cried out against the altar by the word of the Lord, and said, "O altar, altar! Thus says the Lord: 'Behold, a child, Josiah by name, shall be born to the house of David; and on you he shall sacrifice the priests of the high places who burn incense on you, and men's bones shall be burned on you.'" And he gave a sign the same day, saying, "This is the sign which the Lord has spoken: Surely the altar shall split apart, and the ashes on it shall be poured out."
>
> -1 Kings 13:1-3

In hearing this prophetic word, King Jeroboam stretches out his hand against this prophet to have him arrested and the king's hand shrivels up as he does so. The altar also splits open and the ashes spill out. Horrified, the king asks the prophet to entreat the Lord to have his hand restored. The prophet does so, and the king's hand is made normal again. Then King Jeroboam wants the prophet to come back to the king's house to eat and be refreshed.

> But the man of God said to the king, "If you were to give me half your house, I would not go in with you; nor would I eat bread nor drink water in this place. For so it was commanded me by the word of the Lord, saying, 'You shall not eat bread, nor drink water, nor return by the same way you came.'" So he went another way and did not return by the way he came to Bethel.
>
> -1 Kings 13:8-10

So, this prophet has clear instructions from God about what he is to do (and not do), what he is to say, and even how he is to journey, and after he completes his assignment, he departs to head home to Judah. Now, some young men were observing all the events that happened in Bethel, and they went home and told their father, who also was a prophet, all that had taken place. Upon hearing this, the old prophet inquires which direction this man went, and he goes after the unnamed prophet from Judah and stops him on the road.

> Then he said to his sons, "Saddle the donkey for me." So they saddled the donkey for him; and he rode on it, and went after the man of God, and found him sitting under an oak. Then he said to him, "Are you the man of God who came from Judah?" And he said, "I am." Then he said to him, "Come home with me and eat bread." And he said, "I cannot return with you nor go in with you; neither can I eat bread nor drink water with you in this place. For I have been told by the word of the Lord, 'You shall not eat bread nor drink water there, nor return by going the way you came.'" He said to him, "I too am a prophet as you are, and an angel spoke to me by the word of the Lord, saying, 'Bring him back with you to your house, that he may eat bread and drink water.'" (He was lying to him.) So he went back with him, and ate bread in his house, and drank water.
>
> -1 Kings 13:13-19

While the unnamed prophet from Judah is eating and drinking at the old prophet's house, the old prophet receives the word of the Lord as well.

> Now it happened, as they sat at the table, that the word of the Lord came to the prophet who had brought him back; and he cried out to the man of God who came from Judah,

saying, "Thus says the Lord: 'Because you have disobeyed the word of the Lord, and have not kept the commandment which the Lord your God commanded you, but you came back, ate bread, and drank water in the place of which the Lord said to you, "Eat no bread and drink no water," your corpse shall not come to the tomb of your fathers.'" So it was, after he had eaten bread and after he had drunk, that he saddled the donkey for him, the prophet whom he had brought back. When he was gone, a lion met him on the road and killed him. And his corpse was thrown on the road, and the donkey stood by it. The lion also stood by the corpse. And there, men passed by and saw the corpse thrown on the road, and the lion standing by the corpse. Then they went and told it in the city where the old prophet dwelt.

-1 Kings 13:20-25

This is a terrible ending for this prophet from Judah, but it illustrates to us perfectly the failure to be submitted to authority even when on a successful assignment from the Lord. We don't know why the old prophet pursued the unnamed prophet in the first place, but he found him resting under a tree. The unnamed prophet initially refuses the old prophet's hospitality for the same reasons he refused the king's offer, so he knew in his heart what was right and what was wrong. The old prophet then uses deception to trick the unnamed prophet. The Bible does not tell us why the old prophet lied to him. Perhaps he was moved with human compassion for the unnamed prophet, in that, perhaps the unnamed prophet looked wearied from travel and in need of refreshment. Regardless of the reason, the old prophet was dishonest, spoke a false word, and even claimed it came by angelic revelation. And instead of the unnamed prophet doing what he knew in his heart was the right thing to do, he disobeyed and went to the old prophet's house.

The true word of the Lord comes to the deceptive old prophet, and he pronounces significant judgment on this unnamed prophet. Notice several things: the deceptive prophet, who sinned, was still able to prophesy the true word of the Lord; the unnamed prophet was not excused from his disobedience to the Lord because he was lied to; and finally, when the unnamed prophet was disobedient to the Lord, he exhausted his usefulness as a prophet. If this was a test of the Lord, the unnamed prophet failed with significant consequences. Even the claim of angelic revelation was not an excuse. If we receive the word of the Lord, then there is no other authority that can change what was said to us. Now, I realize that is a dangerous implication to make, because it gives the rebel, the perfect excuse, "the Lord told me…". But in reality, it is not an excuse at all. This principle is held in balance and tension with the totality of Scripture. In other words, we need to have more than "the Lord told me…" if what the Lord told us is going to cause rebellion, because the Lord is not going to violate other parts of His holy Word to give you an excuse to rebel. God's Word cannot contradict, or He would be contradicting Himself. So He will not give us a directive, mission, or assignment that will cause us to be in rebellion to delegated authority unless it is for a reason of disobedience that He sanctions in His Word, which we will cover in Chapter 12.

So when Josiah learns that this grave he sees belongs to the unnamed prophet who prophesied Josiah's reforms, he instructs his servants to leave it be, but the altar is destroyed as the unnamed prophet prophesied a few hundred years before.

Now Josiah also took away all the shrines of the high places that were in the cities of Samaria, which the kings of Israel had made to provoke the Lord to anger; and he did to them according to all the deeds he had done in Bethel. He executed all the priests of the high places who were there, on the altars, and burned men's bones on them; and he returned to Jerusalem. "Then the king commanded all the people, saying, "Keep the Passover to the Lord your God, as it is written in this Book of the Covenant." Such a Passover surely had never been held since the days of the judges who judged Israel, nor in all the days of the kings of Israel and the kings of Judah. But in the eighteenth year of King Josiah this Passover was held before the Lord in Jerusalem. Moreover Josiah put away those who consulted mediums and spiritists, the household gods and idols, all the abominations that were seen in the land of Judah and in Jerusalem, that he might perform the words of the law which were written in the book that Hilkiah the priest found in the house of the Lord. Now before him there was no king like him, who turned to the Lord with all his heart, with all his soul, and with all his might, according to all the Law of Moses; nor after him did any arise like him.

-2 Kings 23:19-25

So, Josiah is killing it, right? Following hard after God, putting into place everything he is supposed to, leading the nation in the right direction, and the Bible testifies that there was no king before who was ever like him. No king had ever turned his heart to the Lord with all his heart, soul, and strength, and none came after him either that would do that. Wow! What a statement, considering some of the kings who came before him, like David, for example. What an honor for King Josiah! Now verses 28-30 of 2 Kings 23, tell the story of the death of Josiah, but they leave out the details. To get them we have to go over to

2 Chronicles. In chapter 35, we pick up with this story of the Passover.

So all the service of the Lord was prepared the same day, to keep the Passover and to offer burnt offerings on the altar of the Lord, according to the command of King Josiah. And the children of Israel who were present kept the Passover at that time, and the Feast of Unleavened Bread for seven days. There had been no Passover kept in Israel like that since the days of Samuel the prophet; and none of the kings of Israel had kept such a Passover as Josiah kept, with the priests and the Levites, all Judah and Israel who were present, and the inhabitants of Jerusalem. In the eighteenth year of the reign of Josiah this Passover was kept. After all this, when Josiah had prepared the temple, Necho king of Egypt came up to fight against Carchemish by the Euphrates; and Josiah went out against him. But he sent messengers to him, saying, "What have I to do with you, king of Judah? I have not come against you this day, but against the house with which I have war; for God commanded me to make haste. Refrain from meddling with God, who is with me, lest He destroy you." Nevertheless Josiah would not turn his face from him, but disguised himself so that he might fight with him, and did not heed the words of Necho from the mouth of God. So he came to fight in the Valley of Megiddo. And the archers shot King Josiah; and the king said to his servants, "Take me away, for I am severely wounded." His servants therefore took him out of that chariot and put him in the second chariot that he had, and they brought him to Jerusalem. So he died, and was buried in one of the tombs of his fathers. And all Judah and Jerusalem mourned for Josiah. Jeremiah also lamented for Josiah. And to this day all the singing men and the singing women speak of Josiah in their lamentations. They made it a custom in Israel; and indeed they are written in the Laments. Now the rest of the acts of Josiah and his goodness, according to what was written in the Law of the Lord, and his deeds from first to last, indeed they are written in the book of the kings of Israel and Judah.

-2 Chronicles 35:16-27

And that is the sad, sad ending to the most righteous king who ever lived, according to the Bible. More righteous than David. Restores true worship to the Kingdom of Judah. No recorded sins. No scandals. No failures. No departure from the Lord to the right or the left. What happened? He took up the cause of the Lord, or so he thought. The Bible does not dispute King Necho of Egypt's claim, that he was commanded by God to go make war with Carchemish. But here comes Josiah, thinking he is doing the Lord's work, by keeping those pesky foreigners in check. He's told that Pharaoh is on assignment from God, but he does not listen. Instead, he decides to go out and pick a fight, because after all, it is not possible the Lord is with Pharaoh. After all, the Lord would naturally be on the side of the most righteous king who ever lived right?!

It was even prophesied over him by Huldah, that he would go down to his grave in peace, so he had a prophetic destiny! But he died in war, with an arrow to the chest. That doesn't look like peace to me! What happened? Was the prophet wrong? Was the prophecy not the word of the Lord? It was the word of the Lord and the prophet was not wrong! But an aspect of prophecy that most Christians hate to consider is that prophecy is conditional. We must partner with the word of the Lord over our lives. And if He says we'll go down to our grave in peace, then we cannot go around looking to pick a fight in something that is none of our business!

Yes, Josiah was a righteous king with a prophetic destiny, and yes the Lord was with him in everything he did. That is until that righteous king got in the way of what the Lord was accomplishing through someone else. Then he got an arrow to the chest.

Sadly, this is the same excuse used by Christians throughout the church today. "You cannot tell me what to do, God told me such and such, the Lord is on my side …".

Not everyone who says to Me, "Lord, Lord," shall enter the kingdom of heaven, *but he who does the will of My Father in heaven* [emphasis mine]. Many will say to Me in that day, "Lord, Lord, have we not prophesied in Your name, cast out demons in Your name, and done many wonders in Your name?" And then I will declare to them, "I never knew you; depart from Me, you who practice *lawlessness* [rebellion]!"

-Matthew 7:21-23

12
OUR DUTY TO DISOBEY

Shadrach, Meshach, and Abed-Nego answered and said to the king,
"O Nebuchadnezzar, we have no need to answer you in this matter.
If that is the case, our God whom we serve is able to deliver us from the burning
fiery furnace, and He will deliver us from your hand, O king.
But if not, let it be known to you, O king, that we don't serve your gods,
nor will we worship the gold image which you have set up."
-Daniel 3:16-18

Now by this point, maybe you think I am crazy. I can hear
you now, "There has got to be a time when it is okay to disobey,
especially if the person or authority I am disobeying is evil and
wicked." Well, I have good news for you that will satisfy that
rebel heart. There are occasions where the Lord sanctions
disobedience to delegated authority, but not many. So, what are
the occasions for civil disobedience or disobedience to delegated
authority?

There are three general positions on civil disobedience: The
anarchist says people can defy the government whenever they
want, and their only justification is how they feel about it.
Clearly, there is no biblical support for that position in light of
Romans 13. The extremist patriot who says people should
always follow the state or country no matter what. That gets
sticky when the natural laws of man run afoul of the laws of

God. So, the last position we are left with then is the biblical position of submission, which is that a Christian can act out in civil disobedience only if the government commands evil.

There are only eight examples of civil disobedience in Scripture that are sanctioned by God. Five of them involve the murder of innocents.

1. Exodus 1 – the command by Pharaoh to kill Jewish baby boys. Verse 17 says God was good to the midwives because they feared God more than Pharaoh.
2. Joshua 2 – Rahab disobeyed the king of Jericho concerning hiding the Israelite spies which would have meant their death.
3. 1 Samuel 14 – King Saul orders no one to eat until they are victorious in the battle over the Philistines. Jonathan unknowingly eats, but the people resist Saul and Jonathan is spared.
4. 1 Kings 18 – Obadiah hid 100 of the Lord's prophets from Jezebel to save them from death.
5. 2 Kings 11 – Joash is hidden by Jehoida because king Ahaziah's mother is killing off all of the royal offspring of Judah.

The next three instances of sanctioned disobedience involve the worship of a deity other than God or commands to stop preaching Jesus.

6. Daniel 3 - Shadrach, Meshach, and Abednego refuse to bow to the idol of Nebuchadnezzar.
7. Acts 4 and 5 – Peter and John refuse to stop preaching in the name of Jesus Christ.
8. Revelation 13 – refusal by Christians to worship the image of the Antichrist.

These are the only occasions in Scripture where the characters are people of God, and the Lord looks favorably on their disobedience to authority. That is a staggeringly short list for a book that is as rich and comprehensive as the Bible is. That fact alone should tell us what God thinks of disobedience and rebellion. In instances like these, and only in instances like these, we must disobey the earthly authorities and appeal to the ultimate authority, God. If it means we die as a result, God is okay with that outcome.

13

JESUS, THE MAN OF AUTHORITY

Then He went down with them and came to Nazareth, and was subject to them, but His mother kept all these things in her heart.
-Luke 2:51

Now we will examine the authority of Jesus Christ. What do we mean by the authority of Jesus Christ? Does it mean being in charge? No, having authority and being in charge are not the same thing. We are talking about more than that. We are talking about the right of Jesus Christ to speak and act on His Father's behalf in forgiving sin, pronouncing judgment, and promising eternal life to those who believe in Him.

To rightly understand authority or get the clearest picture of it, we need to look at the life of Jesus. Submission and authority are related, and we cannot have one without the other. Now I need to clarify something when I say that because I am not talking about conduct. The measure of the authority we are entrusted with is directly related to our ability to be submitted to authority, so when I say that we cannot have one without the other, that is what I mean. You as an individual cannot walk in authority without walking in submission. We cannot and will not be trusted with authority if we will not be submitted to authority. In fact, **to the degree that we desire authority, we must be submitted to authority.** Want to have greater authority over sickness and disease? Walk in greater submission. Want to have greater authority over the things in the spiritual realm? Walk in greater submission. See, it is counter to the culture. People equate rulership, authority, and power with being in charge. No! Authority is submission and serving. The greater the submission, the greater the authority, rulership, and power. Many people don't like the idea of being submitted to authority. Some are mildly rebellious and some live in the woods hatching plans against the government, declaring everything but themselves as evil tyrants. But the truth is that everyone is submitted to authority to one degree or another. See even the 'patriot' who has no regard for governmental authority, still stops at the red light when he comes to town for supplies. In some way shape or form, everyone is submitted. The question is how much are we submitted? Jesus was all-powerful as a man because He was completely submitted and obedient as a man. Having no sin is not what gave Jesus His power to heal; having no sin is what made Jesus worthy to be an atonement for all of man for all time. Hence the reason your ability and power to heal has nothing to do with the sin habit in your life or absence thereof. That is why sometimes we see leaders in the Body of Christ, living in secret sin, but still able to minister in their gifting. Their abilities are not sin-based. Sure, living in sin will eventually expose them and ruin their destiny, but their gift will still function.

It was Jesus' submission and obedience to the Father that gave Him authority. In the years from 12 to 30, He learned it, like everyone else has to learn it. Luke 2:41-52 states,

> Now His parents went to Jerusalem every year at the Feast of the Passover. And when He was twelve years old, they

went up according to custom. And when the feast was ended, as they were returning, the boy Jesus stayed behind in Jerusalem. His parents did not know it, but supposing Him to be in the group they went a day's journey, but then they began to search for Him among their relatives and acquaintances, and when they did not find Him, they returned to Jerusalem, searching for Him. After three days they found Him in the temple, sitting among the teachers, listening to them and asking them questions. And all who heard Him were amazed at His understanding and His answers. And when His parents saw Him, they were astonished. And His mother said to Him, "Son, why have You treated us so? Behold, Your father and I have been searching for You in great distress." And He said to them, "Why were you looking for Me? Did you not know that I must be in My Father's house?" And they did not understand the saying that He spoke to them. And He went down with them and came to Nazareth and was submissive to them. And His mother treasured up all these things in her heart. And Jesus increased in wisdom and in stature and in favor with God and man.

-Luke 2:41-52

In the next chapter of Luke, Jesus is 30 years old and getting baptized. Eighteen years, people. What was He doing for 18 years? He was not sitting around wasting time or twiddling His thumbs. I believe He was learning submission and obedience. When He was 30, I believe He had reached a place where He had demonstrated that He was submitted, obedient, trustworthy, and ready for ministry ... and then He was tested along those lines to make sure.

Then Jesus, being filled with the Holy Spirit, returned from the Jordan and was led by the Spirit into the wilderness, being tempted for forty days by the devil. And in those days He ate nothing, and afterward, when they had ended, He was hungry. And the devil said to Him, "If You are the Son of God, command this stone to become bread." But Jesus answered him, saying, "It is written, 'Man shall not live by bread alone, but by every word of God.'" Then the devil, taking Him up on a high mountain, showed Him all the kingdoms of the world in a moment of time. And the devil said to Him, "All this authority I will give You, and their glory; for this has been delivered to me, and I give it to whomever I wish. Therefore, if You will worship before me, all will be Yours." And Jesus answered and said to him, "Get behind Me, Satan! For it is written, 'You shall worship the Lord your God, and Him only you shall serve.'" Then he brought Him to Jerusalem, set Him on the pinnacle of the temple, and said to Him, "If You are the Son of God, throw Yourself down from here. For it is written: 'He shall give His angels charge over you, To keep you,' and 'In their hands they shall bear you up, Lest you dash your foot against a stone.'" And Jesus answered and said to him, "It has been said, 'You shall not tempt the Lord your God.'" Now when the devil had ended every temptation, he departed from Him until an opportune time. Then Jesus returned in the power of the Spirit to Galilee, and news of Him went out through all the surrounding region. And He taught in their synagogues, being glorified by all.

-Luke 4:1-15

Jesus was tested to see if His obedience was token or genuine. Now you may say that's ridiculous, but if not, then what was the point of the test? For looks? Listen, we can obey and not be submitted, just as we can be submitted and not obey (see the parable of the man with two sons, Matthew 21:28-33). One is an attitude, and one is conduct. They are not the same thing. Testing and trial are what brings it out of us and reveals

174

our hearts. Jesus demonstrated in the face of severe testing, both His submission, or heart attitude, and His obedience, or His conduct. Then His ministry was anointed by the power of the Holy Spirit and it began. Notice that in Luke 4:14, after His testing, "Jesus returned in the power of the Spirit to Galilee."

In Matthew 8, Jesus had demonstrated to the Father that He was ready, willing, and able to be trusted with the highest levels of authority. What level of authority did Jesus walk in? Let's look at a few examples. First, Jesus demonstrated His authority over nature.

> Now when He got into a boat, His disciples followed Him. And suddenly a great tempest arose on the sea, so that the boat was covered with the waves. But He was asleep. Then His disciples came to Him and awoke Him, saying, "Lord, save us! We are perishing!" But He said to them, "Why are you fearful, O you of little faith?" Then He arose and rebuked the winds and the sea, and there was a great calm. So the men marveled, saying, "Who can this be, that even the winds and the sea obey Him?"
>
> -Matthew 8:23-27

In the next chapter, Jesus demonstrated His authority over sin and sickness.

> So He got into a boat, crossed over, and came to His own city. Then behold, they brought to Him a paralytic lying on a bed. When Jesus saw their faith, He said to the paralytic, "Son, be of good cheer; your sins are forgiven you." And at once some of the scribes said within themselves, "This Man blasphemes!" But Jesus, knowing their thoughts, said, "Why do you think evil in your hearts? For which is easier, to say, '*Your* sins are forgiven you,' or

to say, 'Arise and walk'? But that you may know that the Son of Man has power on earth to forgive sins"—then He said to the paralytic, "Arise, take up your bed, and go to your house." And he arose and departed to his house. Now when the multitudes saw *it*, they marveled and glorified God, who had given such power to men."

-Matthew 9:1-8

Jesus also demonstrated His authority over death.

While He spoke these things to them, behold, a ruler came and worshiped Him, saying, "My daughter has just died, but come and lay Your hand on her and she will live." So Jesus arose and followed him, and so did His disciples. And suddenly, a woman who had a flow of blood for twelve years came from behind and touched the hem of His garment. For she said to herself, "If only I may touch His garment, I shall be made well." But Jesus turned around, and when He saw her He said, "Be of good cheer, daughter; your faith has made you well." And the woman was made well from that hour. When Jesus came into the ruler's house, and saw the flute players and the noisy crowd wailing, He said to them, "Make room, for the girl is not dead, but sleeping." And they ridiculed Him. But when the crowd was put outside, He went in and took her by the hand, and the girl arose.

-Matthew 9:18-25

Jesus also demonstrated His power over evil. Mark 1:23-27,

Now there was a man in their synagogue with an unclean spirit. And he cried out, saying, "Let us alone! What have we to do with You, Jesus of Nazareth? Did You come to destroy us? I know who You are—the Holy One of God!" But Jesus rebuked him, saying, "Be quiet, and come out of him!" And when the unclean spirit had convulsed him and cried out with a loud voice, he came out of him. Then they were all amazed, so that they questioned among themselves, saying, "What is this? What new doctrine is this? For with authority He commands even the unclean spirits, and they obey Him."

-Mark 1:23-27

The level of authority Jesus had was incredible. It was the level of authority where there is no failure rate when interacting with nature, the sick, death, or demonic power. This does not mean that Jesus was then free to do whatever He wanted, even though He had attained that level of authority. Submission is continual. That level of authority also meant that He had attained that level of submission. The reason Jesus' healings never failed to take place is that He never attempted to do anything outside of permission from the Father. John 8:28, "Then Jesus said to them, "When you lift up the Son of Man, then you will know that I am He, and that I do nothing of Myself; but as My Father taught Me, I speak these things."

Some translations read, "I do nothing of my own initiative." Now, all-powerful Jesus could deal with nature, any sickness, disease, death, or demonic power, and yet He still says, "I do nothing of my own initiative." How many of us, if we had those same abilities, that measure of authority, would not walk down to the local hospital and go floor by floor, room by room, and clean it out? Heal everybody, send the doctors and nurses home, we got this! That is what Jesus would want us to do is it not? I am not so sure. See, Jesus, having all of the access, to all of the power He needed, to do any miracle in the world, did not confuse His power and authority with permission. "I do nothing of my own initiative." I know some of you don't believe me. Let

177

us go back to John 5 to see if I can prove my point.

> After this there was a feast of the Jews, and Jesus went up to Jerusalem. Now there is in Jerusalem by the Sheep Gate a pool, which is called in Hebrew, Bethesda, having five porches. In these lay a great multitude of sick people, blind, lame, paralyzed, waiting for the moving of the water. For an angel went down at a certain time into the pool and stirred up the water; then whoever stepped in first, after the stirring of the water, was made well of whatever disease he had. Now a certain man was there who had an infirmity thirty-eight years. When Jesus saw him lying there, and knew that he already had been in that condition a long time, He said to him, "Do you want to be made well?" The sick man answered Him, "Sir, I have no man to put me into the pool when the water is stirred up; but while I am coming, another steps down before me." Jesus said to him, "Rise, take up your bed and walk." And immediately the man was made well, took up his bed, and walked. And that day was the Sabbath.
>
> -John 5:1-9

Now beginning in verse 10-16, you have the Jews mad at this newly healed guy, because he is carrying his bed on the Sabbath. Always great to have the religious folks around to point out why you should not be doing something.

> But Jesus answered them, "My Father has been working until now, and I have been working." Therefore the Jews sought all the more to kill Him, because He not only broke the Sabbath, but also said that God was His Father, making Himself equal with God. Then Jesus answered and said to them, "Most assuredly, I say to you, the Son can do nothing of Himself, but what He sees the Father do; for whatever He does, the Son also does in like manner. For the Father loves the Son, and shows Him all things that He

Himself does; and He will show Him greater works than these, that you may marvel. For as the Father raises the dead and gives life to them, even so the Son gives life to whom He will. For the Father judges no one, but has committed all judgment to the Son, that all should honor the Son just as they honor the Father. He who does not honor the Son does not honor the Father who sent Him. "Most assuredly, I say to you, he who hears My word and believes in Him who sent Me has everlasting life, and shall not come into judgment, but has passed from death into life. Most assuredly, I say to you, the hour is coming, and now is, when the dead will hear the voice of the Son of God; and those who hear will live. For as the Father has life in Himself, so He has granted the Son to have life in Himself, and has given Him authority to execute judgment also, because He is the Son of Man. Don't marvel at this; for the hour is coming in which all who are in the graves will hear His voice and come forth—those who have done good, to the resurrection of life, and those who have done evil, to the resurrection of condemnation. I can of Myself do nothing. As I hear, I judge; and My judgment is righteous, because I don't seek My own will but the will of the Father who sent Me. "If I bear witness of Myself, My witness is not true. There is another who bears witness of Me, and I know that the witness which He witnesses of Me is true. You have sent to John, and he has borne witness to the truth. Yet I don't receive testimony from man, but I say these things that you may be saved. He was the burning and shining lamp, and you were willing for a time to rejoice in his light. But I have a greater witness than John's; for the works which the Father has given Me to finish—the very works that I do—bear witness of Me, that the Father has sent Me. And the Father Himself, who sent Me, has testified of Me. You have neither heard His voice at any time, nor seen His form. But you don't have His word abiding in you, because whom He sent, Him you don't believe. You search the Scriptures, for in them you think you have eternal life; and these are they which testify of Me. But you are not willing to come to Me that you may have life."

-John 5:17-40

So, in verse 3 it says "a multitude of invalids." A multitude. When the Jews got on the case of the man who was carrying his bed and he said, "I am only carrying it because the guy who healed me told me to carry it," they asked, "Who told you to carry it?" Verse 13 says, "But the one who was healed did not know who it was, for Jesus had withdrawn, a multitude being in that place." So, there is a multitude of invalids and a crowd ... and Jesus heals ONE guy. "I do nothing of my own initiative." Are we so submitted that we could carry the anointing of Jesus and walk through that crowd and heal ONE guy and to the rest of the crowd say, "I do nothing of my own initiative"? Didn't Jesus see the need? He had to have seen the need. Didn't Jesus have compassion? Of course He had compassion. Didn't Jesus want everyone to be healed? Of course He wanted everyone to be healed. But He does nothing of His own initiative, which is most often our problem. We're always about our initiative, instead of His. I am convinced beyond all measure that if God the Father told Jesus to heal every person in that place that Jesus would have taken as long as needed to heal every single person. Why God chooses some to be healed and not others are part of the mystery of His will. One day we'll have the answer, but in the meantime, it's not our place to judge or have evil suspicions about the Lord.

The Greek term for authority, in both the NT and the Septuagint, is *exousia*. *Exousia* is sometimes translated as "power," but *exousia* in Greek typically does not refer to physical strength or power even though it is translated as "power." "Power" is more accurately translated from the Greek word *dunamis*, but *exousia* means, or translates to, "the rightful and legitimate exercise of power." So, because we are talking about a right or legitimacy, a person has authority primarily by the position one holds, not by physical coercion or might. I wrote on this in Chapter 4. God has intrinsic authority, because of who He is and what He is. His authority is legitimate. That is a crucial element to know and understand. Jesus, in and of Himself, as man, had no power. He did not operate out of power, He operated out of submission and authority. He had laid the power down that He had as God, when He came in the form of man (Philippians 2:7), so power had nothing to do with His ability to perform miracles. That ability had to do with His submission and authority. That is not a denial that He was fully God and fully man. But if He was relying on His deity to do what He did, then He was cheating, and there is no model for us to follow because He would have an unfair advantage that the rest of us cannot have and never attain. Yet He said to His disciples (and to us), "Most assuredly, I say to you, he who believes in Me, the works that I do he will do also; and greater works than these he will do, because I go to My Father" (John 14:12). I believe the "greater" is both in volume and in miraculous power, but if He was cheating by using His powers as a deity, then our hope to follow in His footsteps and do "greater" is a false hope.

The power of God responds to the authority of God. When the power of God is requested it looks for one thing … to see that the request is legitimate and authentic, just as a loyal servant listens for the voice of his master and only his master. Likewise, power is not the question. The power comes in one flavor; it is not a lesser or a greater, it is only power. How do I know it only comes in one flavor? Is Jesus lesser on some days and greater on others? No, He is not.

When children become saved, they do not receive a baby atonement or a baby Holy Spirit. They receive THE atonement and THE Holy Spirit. The same ones an adult receives. There is not a less-than atonement or Holy Spirit, or an immature atonement or Holy Spirit, or an undeveloped atonement or Holy Spirit. Therefore, neither is the power of God underdeveloped, immature, or less-than, because Jesus is the power and wisdom of God.

> For the message of the cross is foolishness to those who are perishing, but to us who are being saved it is the power of God. For it is written: "I will destroy the wisdom of the wise, And bring to nothing the understanding of the prudent." Where is the wise? Where is the scribe? Where is the disputer of this age? Has not God made foolish the wisdom of this world? For since, in the wisdom of God, the world through wisdom did not know God, it pleased God through the foolishness of the message preached to save those who believe. For Jews request a sign, and Greeks seek after wisdom; but we preach Christ crucified, to the Jews a stumbling block and to the Greeks foolishness, but to those who are called, both Jews and Greeks, Christ the power of God and the wisdom of God. Because the foolishness of God is wiser than men, and the weakness of God is stronger than men.
>
> -1 Corinthians 18:25

The power of God is Jesus Christ, and He only comes in one flavor. Jesus is not lesser or greater. The power is not a lesser power or a greater power. How do we see that power manifested in our lives? The Holy Spirit. Luke 24:49, "Behold, I send the Promise of My Father upon you; but tarry in the city of Jerusalem until you are endued with power from on high." Likewise, the Holy Spirit is not a lesser or greater, He is the Holy Spirit. What the power responds to is authority, and authority is what is lesser or greater. The greater the submission AND the obedience, the greater the authority. The greater the authority, the greater the demonstration of power.

This has to do not only with the submission and obedience at the moment but also the submission and obedience in the lifestyle of the person making the request. Jesus operated at the highest level of authority because He was submitted and obedient in His lifestyle. What does that mean? He had regular communion with His Father, and He did what He was told. That was His lifestyle, AND He was submitted and obedient at the moment. Not sometimes one and then the other; both, all the time. The reason man's demonstrations of power in the Holy Spirit fluctuate is that their continual submission to authority fluctuates. Somedays they hit it out of the park with their obedience and somedays they're just rebellious. It happens to all of us; it never happened to Jesus. If the Church wants to have authority—the kind that it prays for all the time—then it starts in the house of obedience. God desires to see every believer operating at the same level that Jesus did. That is one of the reasons why we were created. Ask yourself what would the world look like? Would there be anything withheld from our hands? Would there be anything we could not do for the Kingdom of God? It all comes down to obedience. The Kingdom would not exist without authority, and if we seek to bring the Kingdom to the Earth, if we seek to assist Jesus in returning everything to submission to God, then we must rightly understand, obey, and administer authority in our realm. Satan chose rebellion; what will you choose? The whole world is waiting for your answer.

14

THE PURPOSE OF SUBMISSION AND AUTHORITY

Now when all things are made subject to Him, then the Son Himself will also be subject to Him who put all things under Him, that God may be all in all.
-1 Corinthians 15:28

What on earth are we here for? What is our mission? Yes, I know, to get people saved, live a good life, etc. I know all of the surface answers, but what are the deeper answers? What is God up to? What is His end game and how do we play into that? What is the purpose of our submission and authority?

To understand authority and obedience fully, we must understand the Cross. We must be willing to die; to be obedient to the point of death. Jesus became the ultimate executor of authority because He understood this and embraced it. A major portion of His reward, if you will, is authority.

> Let nothing be done through selfish ambition or conceit, but in lowliness of mind let each esteem others better than himself. Let each of you look out not only for his own interests, but also for the interests of others. Let this mind be in you which was also in Christ Jesus, who, being in the form of God, did not consider it robbery to be equal with God, but made Himself of no reputation, taking the form of a bondservant, and coming in the likeness of men. And being found in appearance as a man, He humbled Himself

and became obedient to the point of death, even the death of the cross. Therefore God also has highly exalted Him and given Him the name which is above every name, that at the name of Jesus every knee should bow, of those in heaven, and of those on earth, and of those under the earth, and that every tongue should confess that Jesus Christ is Lord, to the glory of God the Father.

-Philippians 2:3-11

Jesus proved that He could be trusted with the responsibility of God's authority. And Jesus seeks to share that authority with us. We see this in the sending of the 72 in Luke 10. Upon their return, they were celebrating their accomplishments and Jesus said to them in verse 19, "Behold, I have given you authority to tread on serpents and scorpions, and over all the power of the enemy, and nothing shall hurt you." We also see this repeated in the Great Commission at the end of Matthew's Gospel.

And Jesus came and spoke to them, saying, "All authority has been given to Me in heaven and on earth. Go therefore and make disciples of all the nations, baptizing them in the name of the Father and of the Son and of the Holy Spirit, teaching them to observe all things that I have commanded you; and lo, I am with you always, even to the end of the age.

-Matthew 28:18-20

I wrote earlier in this book that authority is a primary principle of the Kingdom. It is a higher principle than the redemption of man and the problem of sin. I am not minimizing the importance of Christ or what He did; everything He did was vital, but the redemption of man is secondary to the authority of God.

We often say, "It is all about Jesus," and it is; that is a completely true statement. But why is it all about Jesus? Have you ever stopped to consider it? One of the reasons it is all about Jesus is because of His atonement for sin, but that is not the total answer as to why it is all about Jesus. It is all about Jesus because He is the One who brings everything back into subjection to the authority of God. Jesus was the only One who could secure our atonement and forgiveness; thus, He was the only One God could entrust with the authority to bring EVERYTHING back into submission and authority to God. To have dominion on the earth is no small thing, to share in the responsibility of authority is significant, but it even goes beyond the earth. I believe it's everything; the earth, the other planets, the other solar systems; everything, every system, every world God created needs to be brought into subjection! Jesus calls us to Himself so that He might empower us with His authority so that we can rule and reign and assist Him in bringing everything back into subjection to His Father. No other reason. In Revelation 5, Jesus takes the scroll with seven seals from God because He is the only one found worthy to open it. And here's what happens:

> Now when He had taken the scroll, the four living creatures and the twenty-four elders fell down before the Lamb, each having a harp, and golden bowls full of incense, which are the prayers of the saints. And they sang a new song, saying: "You are worthy to take the scroll, And to open its seals; For You were slain, And have redeemed us to God by Your blood, Out of every tribe and tongue and people and nation, And have made us kings and priests to our God; And we shall reign on the earth."
> -Revelation 5:8-10

So, we have been called to reign and rule with Him. It is passages like this that get me fired up when people say to me, "I am not important" or "I don't have anything to contribute." It is one of the greatest lies of the devil. Let me tell you how important you are. You are important enough that He came to die for you, and He wants to empower you with authority and put you in a place of rulership. Whoever you are, despite whatever you have done, He has something for you that He wants you to be an authority over. He would like your assistance in bringing Creation back into order and submission. He is not saving you to save you. Although that is crucial, it is not the chief purpose. He is not saving you to take you to heaven or give you eternal life, although that is important, too. He is saving you, to bring you into a lifestyle of willing obedience and submission, so that He might empower you with authority so that you can rule and reign with Him and be a part of the process of restoring everything to perfect order for His Father. That is what it is all about. And that is why men reject Him. It is not that they don't want the saving, everyone wants to be saved, no one wants to be lost. Everyone wants a King like Jesus. They reject Him because they don't want Him to be Lord. They don't want to submit, because in the recesses of their heart lies rebellion. Jesus came to crush the rebellion and restore order and submission to authority. If you think I am nuts, take a look at this passage:

> For since by man came death, by Man also came the resurrection of the dead. For as in Adam all die, even so in Christ all shall be made alive. But each one in his own order: Christ the firstfruits, afterward those who are Christ's at His coming. Then comes the end, when He

(Jesus) delivers the kingdom to God the Father, when He puts an end to all rule and all authority and power. For He must reign till He has put all enemies under His feet. The last enemy that will be destroyed is death. For "He (God) has put all things under His (Jesus) feet." But when He (God) says "all things are put under Him (Jesus)," it is evident that He (God) who put all things under Him (Jesus) is excepted. Now when all things are made subject to Him (God), then the Son Himself will also be subject to Him (God) who put all things under Him (Jesus), that God may be all in all.

-1 Corinthians 15:21-28

So, in the "end" this all comes down to everything and everyone, except God, coming under complete submission and authority to Jesus. God is King. When everything and everyone is under the authority of Jesus, then Jesus will then subject Himself, and thus everything that is under Him, to God, that God may be all in all. Which is the way things were in the Kingdom before Satan rebelled. Well, how is that for coming full circle?

So, everything is completely restored back to the condition that it was before the foundation of the world, only now there is more that God will be King over than there was at the foundation. Now there is man, and the earth, and all of creation. Jesus undoes or reverses the effects of everything, not just the sin and fall of Adam, but also the rebellion of Satan and the principle of death. God's purpose is about more than man's redemption, it is about more than atonement. It is about the fact that the Kingdom of God was established and in perfect order, and then there arose a rebellion. For some unknown reason God has allowed this rebellion to continue, and He has allowed His creation to live in a state of rebellion for a long time. It is NOT a question of power. Satan is NOT the opposite of God. This is not a Ying and Yang thing. That is what the devil would have you believe. Satan is the opposite of Michael the archangel at best, but he is a created being, so with a breath, God could destroy him and everything he stands for, forever. But in the mystery of His will, God has chosen His Son and man to be part of the restoration plan.

God does not need anything from man, yet He has chosen to use you and me to assist His Son in redeeming His reputation. What do I mean by redeeming God's reputation? What I mean is, Satan rebelled, God could have wiped him out right then, destroyed him forever, game over. But He did not. Why not? I believe it was for His reputation. If God did not deal with Satan's rebellion, His reputation, and His character could be called into question. Why could His reputation and character be called into question if He did not respond? Because God is holy and righteous and in first order, He must be true to Himself. If He did not respond to Satan's rebellion, He would have not been true to Himself.

Satan is called the accuser. How did he get that name? I believe that the moment he was kicked out of heaven he began to curse, blaspheme, and accuse God. He earned his name the accuser. I believe that God was not going to allow Himself to be labeled a dictator or a weakling. He was not going to allow any of the other created beings to have any charge to bring against Him. If He lifted His hand against the devil, He could be accused of being a dictator. If He did nothing, He would be accused of being a weakling or a compromiser. He is neither a dictator nor a weakling. The punishment He imposed on Jesus shows that He is not a weakling, and the forgiveness He provided for us proves that He is a just and loving God.

So instead of wiping out the devil, He set in motion the plan for His Son and mankind, who would willingly choose (the opposite of rebellion) to be submitted and obedient, to destroy the works of the devil. Jesus and those of us that choose His Lordship, prove that we can do what the devil could not do. Man's role is less significant than Jesus' role because Jesus was able to make atonement, but God chose the plan to come to full fruition with man being involved. The Lord has honored us in a way we do not deserve.

When we think critically about this issue, it amazes me that God has even given mankind a role in history at all, but He has. Because Jesus came and modeled what He modeled, we can do the same things Jesus did, "and greater works than these". He also said we have authority over sickness, disease, and even death. So why is there a disconnect? If part of the purpose is for us to walk in authority and power and partner with Jesus to return everything to the way it was before the Fall, then why do we not see more out of the Church today? Why is there a lack of power and authority? Why does the church seem to be losing the war some days?

I am convinced it is due to rebellion and disobedience. In general, I see more rebellious Christians than I see submitted Christians, and if authority is a fundamental issue, and most Christians are being rebellious, then it should be no surprise we have no authority. God is not going to honor people who are rebellious with authority and power. He cannot do it. That would be like honoring Satan, and when we look more like Satan—in our attitude, will, and response—than we look like

Jesus, then we are going nowhere.

In the underground church in China, where they are desperate for God, miracles, signs, and wonders are exploding. People are being raised from the dead. In America, most of what we are raising is offerings, so we can keep our building projects going and keep our coffee shops in the lobby of the church open. And I have nothing against building projects or coffee, but where is the priority of the Church? Are we here to smash the devil and his kingdom in the face and destroy his works, or are we here to have coffee and fellowship?

The Church, the People of God, have yet to realize their importance to the plan and purpose of God. The full power of the Godhead is at our disposal if we could only learn to be a submitted and obedient people. Most of us are wowed and satisfied with the appetizer, but we have no idea, we cannot even conceive, of what God has prepared for us to do on this earth. If we don't humble ourselves and submit to the Lordship of Christ, we will never find out.

I hope that this book will assist everyone who reads it in understanding just how important the principles of submission and authority are, and more importantly the untapped potential that resides within you as a son or daughter of God if you are submitted and obedient. The world is waiting for us to introduce them to the answer, who is Jesus Christ. May the God of all grace bless you and empower you to destroy the works of the devil as you submit to His authority and live obediently to His voice!

15

REBELLION IS EASIER THAN YOU THINK

*Because of rebellion, the Lord's people and the daily sacrifice were given over to it.
It prospered in everything it did, and truth was thrown to the ground.
-Daniel 8:12*

Being rebellious is easier than you think, and while I have spent the majority of this book writing on the importance of avoiding rebellion and being submitted and obedient, what I haven't done is give you practical advice. I said earlier in the book, part of the problem with the church today is: 1) people don't understand what rebellion is—they tend to think of it in terms of crime and illegal activity, 2) they certainly don't think they're rebellious, and 3) they don't conceive that certain behaviors they commit would ever be considered rebellious. So this chapter is about practical things that are rebellious. I've written a short list of things I observe regularly. I would wager that the majority of Christians will read this list and think: a) it is ridiculous, and b) that I'm being legalistic. And that's exactly why we're in the position we're in as the Church at this point. If we honestly meditated on these things, pulled back the veneer, the disillusion, and the deception of the enemy, we would see that while these things appear to be "no big deal" they are in fact demonstrations of rebellion. To put it simply, these are all examples of basic right and wrong, and if they are wrong, then they are rebellious. It's quite simple, but in the age of relativism, and in a time when people spend more time justifying their actions than holding themselves accountable, the devil has wildly deceived people into believing that rebellion is "no big deal". And so long as he keeps us in that posture, thinking that we have freedom, believing in overwhelming grace to justify our sin, then he has us right where he wants us. Because if my hypothesis is true, the vast majority of the Christian church will never walk in the authority and power that God our Father intended, and the devil is perfectly happy with that. And we keep cooperating with him (the devil) willingly...every day. See, he doesn't have to turn us into devil worshippers. He just has to convince us that rebellion, especially in the minor and the mundane of life, is not rebellion. And we can live our lives deceived, being "good" people, just mildly rebellious, we can still make it to heaven (which for most people is their ultimate goal), and meanwhile, we will have lived our lives on earth in a completely powerless way, affecting far less of our world than God intends. That suits the devil just fine, and it suits most Christians just fine because they can live with their conscience, and they will avoid the fires of Hell. So their own selfish, self-centered objectives are met and satisfied, and they go through life inflicting minimal-to-no damage on the kingdom of darkness.

The further I go in life, the more thankful I am for my spiritual inheritance and people like my parents. They didn't sit me down and have talks with me about rebellion. No, they did something far more important. They lived life as Christians, and they meant it. My dad was a pastor, and he was the same man at home as he was at church. I never saw my parents act differently in a different setting. They are people of conviction. Now they weren't perfect, but their conduct was consistent. If something was not right, then it was not right. They weren't tempted to bend the rules or accommodate evil for their gain, EVER, whether there were witnesses or not. They taught me that God sees everything, so the only witness to my conduct that ever mattered was the Almighty. That taught me lessons that I never knew I was learning. For me, the concepts in this book, the principles expressed, are easy to grasp. But as I talk with others and express these views, I'm beginning to see, just how foreign a concept this is for people in the Church. As I said in the introduction, people hear messages on rebellion, and they automatically assign its relevance to things out there, people out there, events out there. They process the message of labeling things rebellious as being reserved for criminals and outrageous conduct, but not for themselves.

And as I shared this book with people so I could get their feedback on what I had written, all of them came back to me and told me how the Lord was already using it to highlight things to them in their lives that they had previously not considered rebellious. All of these people were older than me and have been Christians for longer than I have. Well, I celebrate that God is using the message in their lives, and that's exactly why I'm writing it. So that we all can see where we need further fine-tuning. I want to see people go further than I have in both submission and authority.

But the other thing it's doing is showing lots of people just what the Lord considers rebellion that they have taken for granted. So this chapter has been added as an after-thought. It's a chapter that lists common things that are rebellious that many people take for granted. And I know there will be pushback on what is presented here. People will cry legalism (which is often used as a guise to excuse rebellion). Most people, I find, have no real clue what legalism is, they just think they know. But this is not about legalism. We need to get things right. And despite what the postmodern, secular, humanistic culture tells us, there is such a thing as right and wrong. And wrong things are most often rooted in rebellion. And if they're wrong, then we should not be doing them. It's not that hard. It involves discipline and choice.

This is not an all-inclusive list, but I merely present it to get your wheels turning, so that you can begin to consider, just what might be rebellious in your life. Crime, violations of the commands of scripture, they are all givens. This list is more about the "subtle", the "no big deals", the things we do without even thinking we're doing it, and all the while committing rebellion. Some are obvious and ridiculous, and when you read them you'll have no reaction because you'll know right away that they are true, but give some thought to them. Are they things you do without thinking?

Remember, our goal is to look more like Jesus than we did yesterday, to obtain more authority and power in the Holy Spirit so that we can assist Him in bringing everything into submission so that He can return it to God, that God may be all in all.

1. Violating the speed limit.
2. Receiving a package to your house that's not yours, and keeping it.
3. Parking where you shouldn't.
4. Gossip.

5. Parking in a handicap spot using someone else's handicap permit.
6. Telling people you will pray for them when you have no intention of praying for them.
7. Not filing your taxes, or being dishonest on your taxes so you receive a greater refund.
8. Entering into an establishment's parking lot by driving through the exit, or leaving through the entrance.
9. Receiving too much change back from the cashier and not disclosing it.
10. Rolling through a stop sign.
11. Holding unforgiveness, offense, or bitterness against another person.
12. Using your cell phone while driving in violation of the law.
13. Undermining your leaders.
14. Paying for things in cash or receiving cash for goods or services so you can avoid accountability to the government in the form of taxes or income.
15. Passing someone on the road illegally.
16. Calling in sick to work when you're not.
17. Taking advantage of a program to gain benefits for yourself or others.
18. Checking out at a store, only to realize they didn't properly charge you for your items, and not going back and making it right.
19. Not returning your shopping cart to the corral.
20. Not listening to the instruction of your pastor or other leaders.

How many of those things do you do on a regular basis? How many of those things, and others like them, do you never do? Whatever your answer is, that should give you an indicator of how rebellious or how submitted you are. If you think any one of those things is utterly absurd, then ask yourself honestly if Jesus would do them. If your answer is no, then that means you shouldn't do them either. Jesus was NEVER rebellious, not once, and He died to give us the ability to be the same way.

AFTERWORD

In this book, I presented the idea that our ability to both be submitted and be obedient to God is directly related to, and a major contributor toward, our level of authority as believers in Christ. We progress in authority by posture, serving, humility, avoiding rebellion, being submitted to authority, being repentant, and practicing continual submission as a lifestyle. And all of these things bear their own cost. To whom much is given, much is required (Luke 12:48). After reading everything I have written; I also feel it is appropriate to write what I am not trying to say.

While I wholeheartedly believe in everything I have written as a guide to "success" in authority, these things by themselves are just some of the keys to success. In other words, I am not trying to say that if you only practice these, you will walk in the same level of authority that Jesus walked in. I will say, your level of authority WILL BE significantly increased.

But I must leave room for spiritual maturity, the grace of God, divine wisdom and providence, anointing, calling, and gifting as well. All of those things are also contributors to our level of authority. I think that the majority of what we see in the Body of Christ right now is a reflection of all of those things I just mentioned. The key missing ingredient I believe, is this greater measure of submission and obedience on a wide scale by the Church.

As you may have discerned by my writing, I believe in the operation of the Holy Spirit and the power of God. I believe in the charismata of the Spirit. I believe they have a purpose in the earth, and that purpose has yet to be fulfilled. The discussion for me is a simple one. When Jesus appeared to His disciples after His resurrection, He breathed on them and said, "Receive the Holy Spirit". (John 20:22) He then told them to wait in Jerusalem until they received the gift of the Holy Spirit from His Father. (Acts 1:4) These are two separate acts, two separate instructions, and two separate occasions, to the same disciples. I believe the disciples received salvation in John and the Baptism of the Holy Spirit in Acts so that they would be endued with power from on high to evangelize the lost and destroy the works of Satan. The mission has not changed, and that endowment is still possible for believers today.

I have been supernaturally, physically, healed by God of a torn rotator cuff that needed surgery to repair, as I spent quiet time with Him. And I have had the opportunity to pray for, and lay hands on others who have been healed by the power of God. Thank You, Jesus, and to God be the glory! For me, the issue of power today is not an issue up for discussion because I know intellectually and experientially that God moves in these ways. I continue to see it frequently with my own eyes. No hype, no nonsense, just Jesus at work continually bringing glory to the Father. So, I'm very appreciative of the operation of the Spirit and the gifts, and together they are accomplishing major things in the world. They are being used to destroy the works of the devil, and I wholeheartedly celebrate that. BUT there has to be more.

Even though we see these things in operation on a wide

scale, we are not seeing Jesus-like works by anyone that I am aware of. There are some notables out there, but He said, "and greater works than these" shall we do because He was going to the Father. So where is the greater? I want to see greater in number and greater in scale. And I believe it's coming in a dimension the world has yet to see, but I also feel we need to be prepared in this regard because I want to have a front-row seat AND I want to participate.

I believe the greatest of these works will be performed by the hands of those that are the most submitted, the most obedient, and the most yielded Christians among us. Yes, there will be an element of gifting. Yes, there will be an element of grace. Yes, there will be an element of anointing. Yes, there will be angelic involvement at times. Yes, on some occasions God will sovereignly move through anyone He wants to and do whatever He wants to do. I "yes and amen" all of it. So, it will be a combination of all of these factors and His grace. I just happen to believe our submission and obedience will be one of the biggest contributing factors in the days ahead. In the present era, so many want impartation, but so few want to pay the price. While I love impartation as well, I think it's time we grew up. I think it's time we matured as a Body, and I think it's time we get down to business. We need to put away childish things, we need to mature, and we need to take our obedience seriously.

I do not advocate a mentality that we have to work for it, although it does take work to be submitted and to obey. But we have to do our part, He's already done His. His work is finished. He is seated at the right hand of the Father. It's our turn to receive what He won and get to work bringing everything back into submission.

This is also not a posture of craving authority and power, because, without humility, submission, and obedience, it would destroy us. Too many of us are already casualties of our giftings and callings. We need maturity. This is a posture and approach of being pleasing to the Lord, delighting to do His will, utterly rejecting everything that opposes itself to Him, counting everything as loss for His sake, and being surrendered to His grace.

My prayer for you is that this book has received your attention. If an adjustment to your life is needed to bring you out of rebellion, however mild, so that you look more like Christ as a result, I celebrate that. If you drink in this message of submission and obedience and apply it to your walk, I pray that He moves you from level to level of authority in the Kingdom and you begin to experience the greater works. As more and more believers catch the fire of this message, my prayer is that the Church at large will walk in His authority and power, so that we can assist Jesus in bringing everything into submission, so that it may be presented back to God, that He may be all in all!

I thank you for reading this book. I'll thank you more for applying it, by His grace, and for His everlasting eternal glory. May it be so Lord Jesus, in your mighty, precious, and matchless name! Amen!

NOTES

[1] A.W. Tozer, *The Knowledge of the Holy* (New York: Harper Collins, 1961), 1-2.

[2] All definitions of Bible terms given in this book are adaptations of *Strong's Exhaustive Concordance* and the *Brown-Driver-Briggs* and *Gesenius* lexicons, all of which are available from various online sources.

[3] htttps://www.merriam-webster.com/dictionary/reason.

[4] Watchman Nee, *Spiritual Authority* (New York: Christian Fellowship Publishers, Inc., 1972): 126.

[5] Nee, *Spiritual Authority*, 60.

ACKNOWLEDGMENTS

I would like to thank many people for their support of this work. First, my friend and co-laborer in the Gospel, Dr. Gabriel Miller who painstakingly labored over the manuscript, asked me tough questions, and contributed many hours of his precious time to the final product. Gabriel, I am in your debt.

Next, I would like to thank Philip Pantana, Jr., also my co-laborer in the Gospel, for letting my book challenge him and for agreeing to write the foreword. Philip is a true shepherd and I appreciate his heart towards the flock of God. His compassion is contagious and it helps me to be a better leader.

To those who read my manuscript, gave me constructive criticism, and stayed after me to get it into print, I thank you! Michelle Jolly, your insights were tremendous. Bud Crawford, your critiques were invaluable. Cole Bender, Samuel Petty, and many more, your support and cheerleading were much appreciated. Samuel, your contributions in the arena of graphic design were a real blessing. Thank you, son.

To the people of All Peoples Church, thank you for the honor of leading you in the Way. Your support of me is greatly appreciated and I'm looking forward to spending eternity with all of you!

To my mother Pauline, thank you for your encouragement. You told me since I was a little boy that one day I would be an author. You were right.

To my lovely wife Jessica, and my precious children, Julianna, Jacob, Jamisen, and Joshua, thank you for the many hours of sacrifice you make so dad can do what he's called to do. It's not lost on me what you give. I love you all.

allpeoplesministries

healing • restoration • raising up • sending out

EXPERIENCE THE FULFILLMENT OF YOUR CALLING!

HEALING • RESTORATION • RAISING UP • SENDING OUT

ALL PEOPLES MINISTRIES
PO BOX 3034, LYCHBURG, VA 23403
FOR MORE INFORMATION PLEASE VISIT OUR WEBSITE:
WWW.ALLPEOPLESMINISTRIES.ORG

HOLINESS IS NOT

OPTIONAL!

"The Gospel is this: I used to be evil, but God made a way for me to be good. The Gospel is not this: I used to be evil, but God made a way for me to keep being evil and get away with it."

Holiness is Not Optional is an invitation to rediscover essential truths about the Christian walk, to reclaim our full inheritance of grace, and to release the power of God to transform our lives. A reformation of holiness is upon us. Will you join it?

www.allpeoplesministries.org

Dear Church

A contemporary paraphrase of the New Testament epistles to the Church. Sixteen epistles are included in this volume--Hebrews, 1&2 John, James, Romans, Galatians, Ephesians, Colossians, Philippians, 1&2 Corinthians, 1&2 Thessalonians, 1&2 Peter, and Jude. The paraphrase is designed to be readable without sacrificing important theological terminology. The essence of what God wants to communicate to His people is really brought to the forefront in this work. The book includes discussion questions for a 20-week small-group (or congregational) study.

www.allpeoplesministries.org

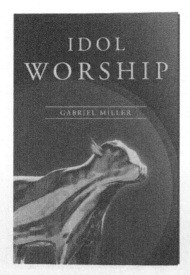

Idol Worship

The American church today is full of idolatry. We may not worship graven images, but we do worship other gods. Most of which we're not even aware of. The gods of our preferences. The gods of our selfish endeavors. When we gather for corporate worship on Sunday mornings, many of us believe we are worshipping God-alone, when we are actually worshipping God-and. God and our idols. Style preference, traditions, even doctrine can be an idol. This book presents 14 "golden calves" that are keeping today's church from its destiny. If we really step back and, for just a moment, stop presuming that we have it all together, the Lord of our lives will reveal to us areas that He wants to correct and purify.

"No other gods! Idol Worship is a prophetic yet humble call of adjustment, one that tears down the high places of the heart and realigns it toward God in genuine worship. What a fresh breath of help for any pastor, leader, worship ministry, and believer!"
- Nancy Clark Vice-President, Mutual Faith Ministries and Network

"This book is both challenging and convicting. Every believer needs to use this tool to evaluate his or her personal worship life."
- Ray Jones, President and Founder, Radiance Ministries

www.allpeoplesministries.org

Worship is more than a style of music. Worship is a lifestyle with several characteristics grounded in the Holy Scripture. This book offers fresh insights into biblical worship. It is concise and can be easily grasped by the Christian community at large, but do not let it's simplicity fool you. Within the pages of this text is a call to come up higher, to think rightly about God and our response to Him, and to live a lifestyle of worship that is worthy of Him.

The
Worship of God

"Miller assembles several significant precious stones of truth into a solid foundation for a life-style and life-time of worship. I urge you not to set this condensed treatise down too long before absorbing it into your spirit and applying it."
- Jeff Clark, President, Mutual Faith Ministries and Network

"Miller's brilliant mind coupled with his tender heart for the Lord and his passion to teach have resulted in the book The Worship of God. I would highly recommend that any student of worship, and every child of God, read this work."
- Fred Guilbert, D.Min, Light Up The Loft Ministries, Former Vice President, Louisiana College

www.allpeoplesministries.org

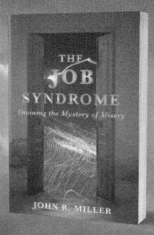

The Job Syndrome

Everyone suffers on some level, but some are forced to endure devastating, life-altering catastrophes. Such was the case for Job, the faithful protagonist of one of the Bible's most peculiar books. His syndrome ranges from shock to anguish to disillusionment to indignation. But in the end it yields a peace and a knowing, a proving and an ascent, to the place where "his spiritual eye sees God as mysteriously holy, triumphantly sovereign and incalculably powerful in all His thoughts and designs, means and ways, purposes and ends." This book is a powerful synthesis of scholarship and pastoral wisdom. A revision of the author's doctoral dissertation specifically tailored to reach clergy and laity alike, Dr. Miller masterfully combines rigorous biblical scholarship with real-life stories and practical application to present us with a valuable guide for coping with calamity. *This book contains true stories of tragic events that may be too intense for younger readers.

www.allpeoplesministries.org

Advice on Finding & Keeping a Wife

This coffee-table book contains 70 nuggets of wisdom for both young men in search of a wife and those who are already married. At a time when the culture around us screams "me, myself, and I," it is important to return to common-sense principles and scriptural values that show us that giving, serving, and selfless love are at the core of successful relationships.

www.allpeoplesministries.org

Worship Music from APM!

Purchase on our website!

www.allpeoplesministries.org

Worship Music from APM!

Purchase on our website!

www.allpeoplesministries.org

Worship Music from APM!

Purchase on our website!

www.allpeoplesministries.org

Worship Music from APM!

Purchase on our website!

www.allpeoplesministries.org

Coming Soon from APM!

Purchase on our website!

65180200R00126